THIS BOOK BELONGS TO:

Copyright © 2021 *Michael Blackmore*

All rights reserved.

No parts of this publication may be reproduced, distributed, or transmitted in any form, or by any means, including photocopying, recording, or other electronic or mechanical methods, without prior written permission from the publisher.

HOW MANY SANTAS DO YOU SEE?

★ MERRY CHRISTMAS

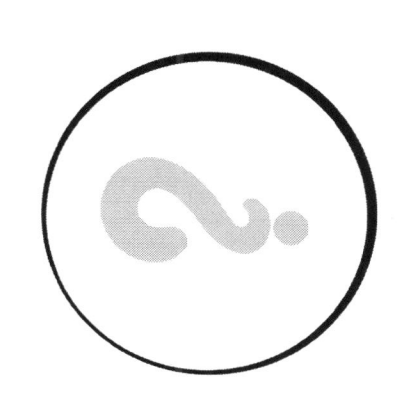

FIND
7
DIFFERENCES

HOW MANY?

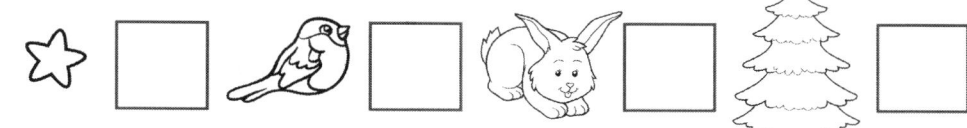

FIND
10
DIFFERENCES

FIND
7
DIFFERENCES

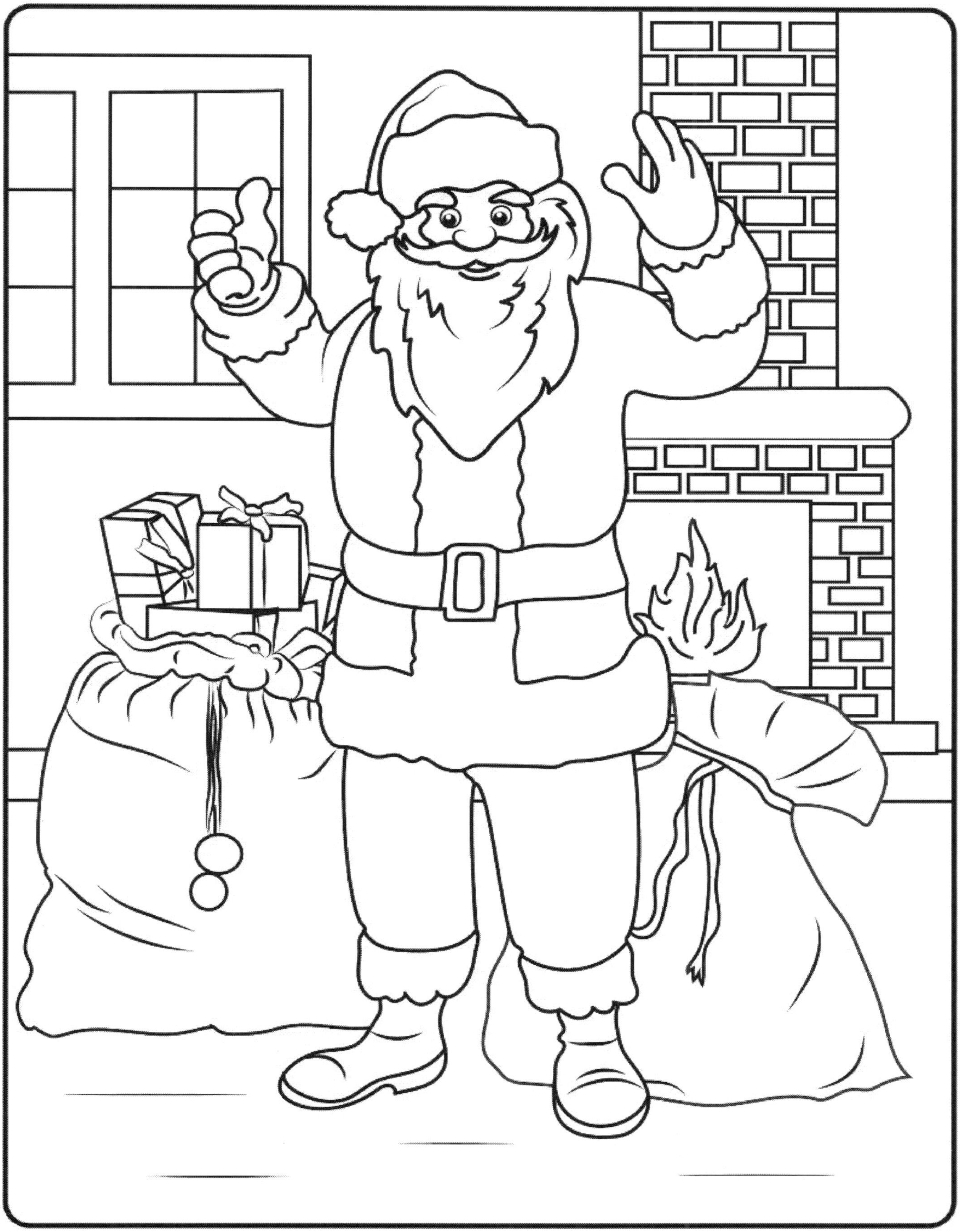

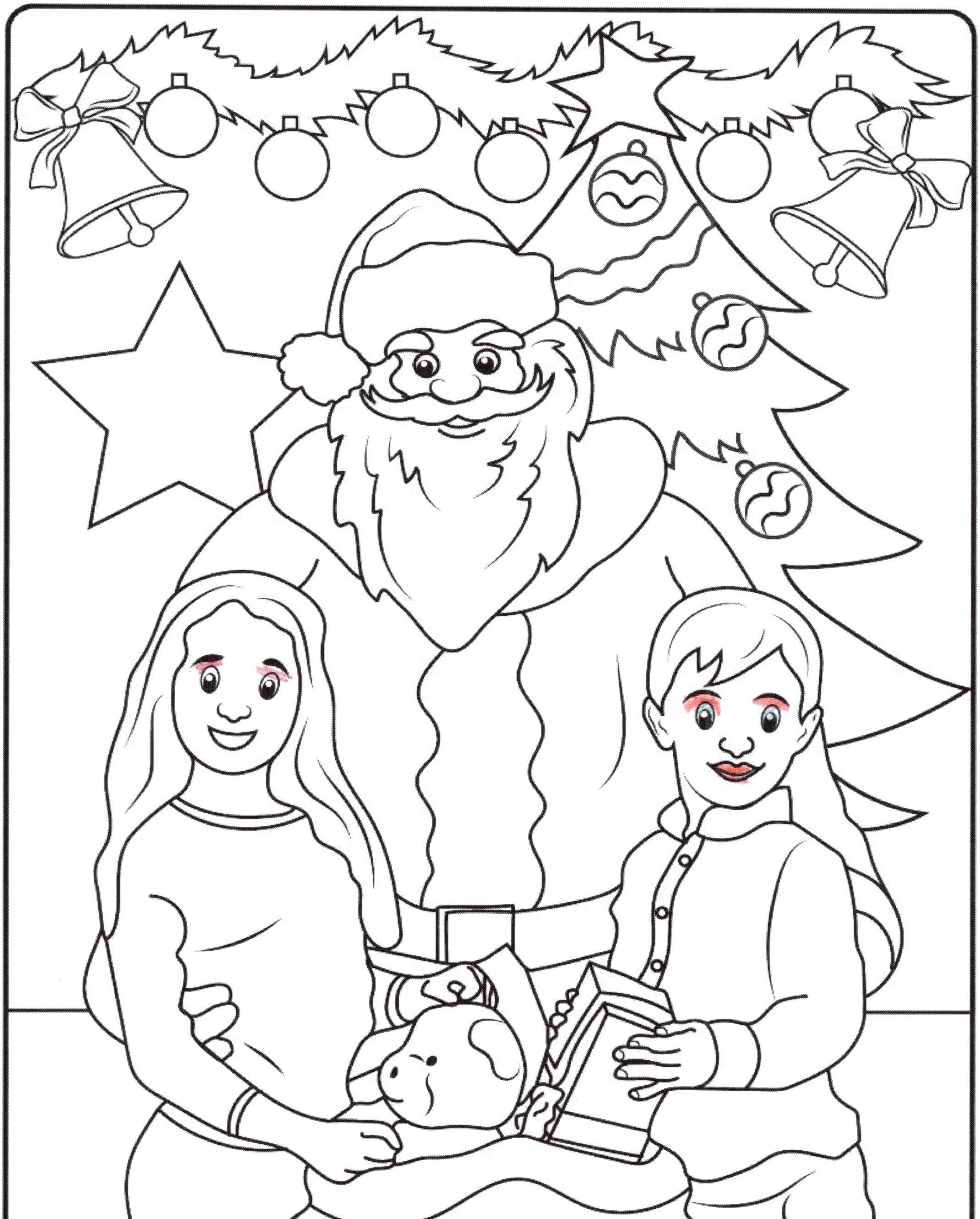

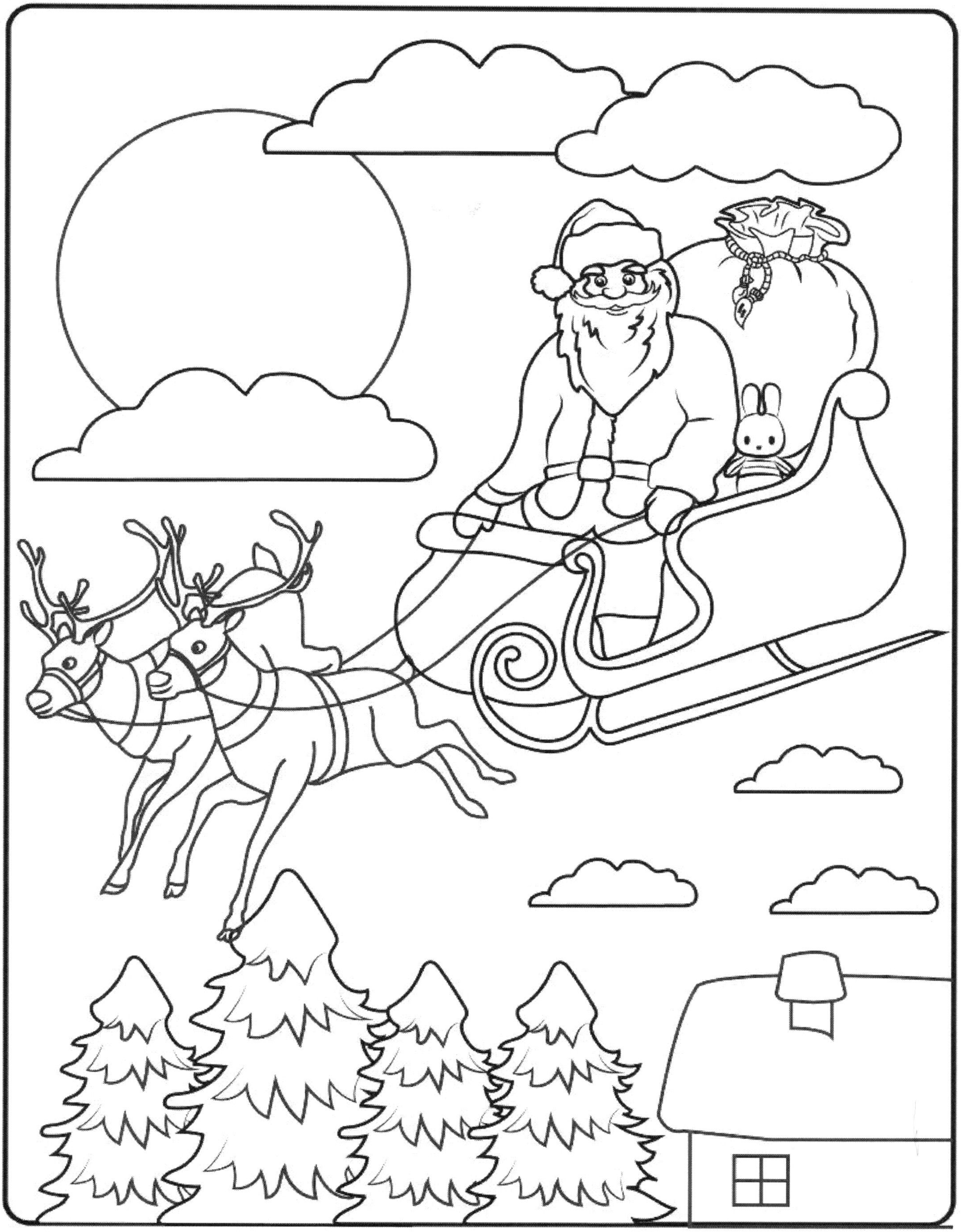

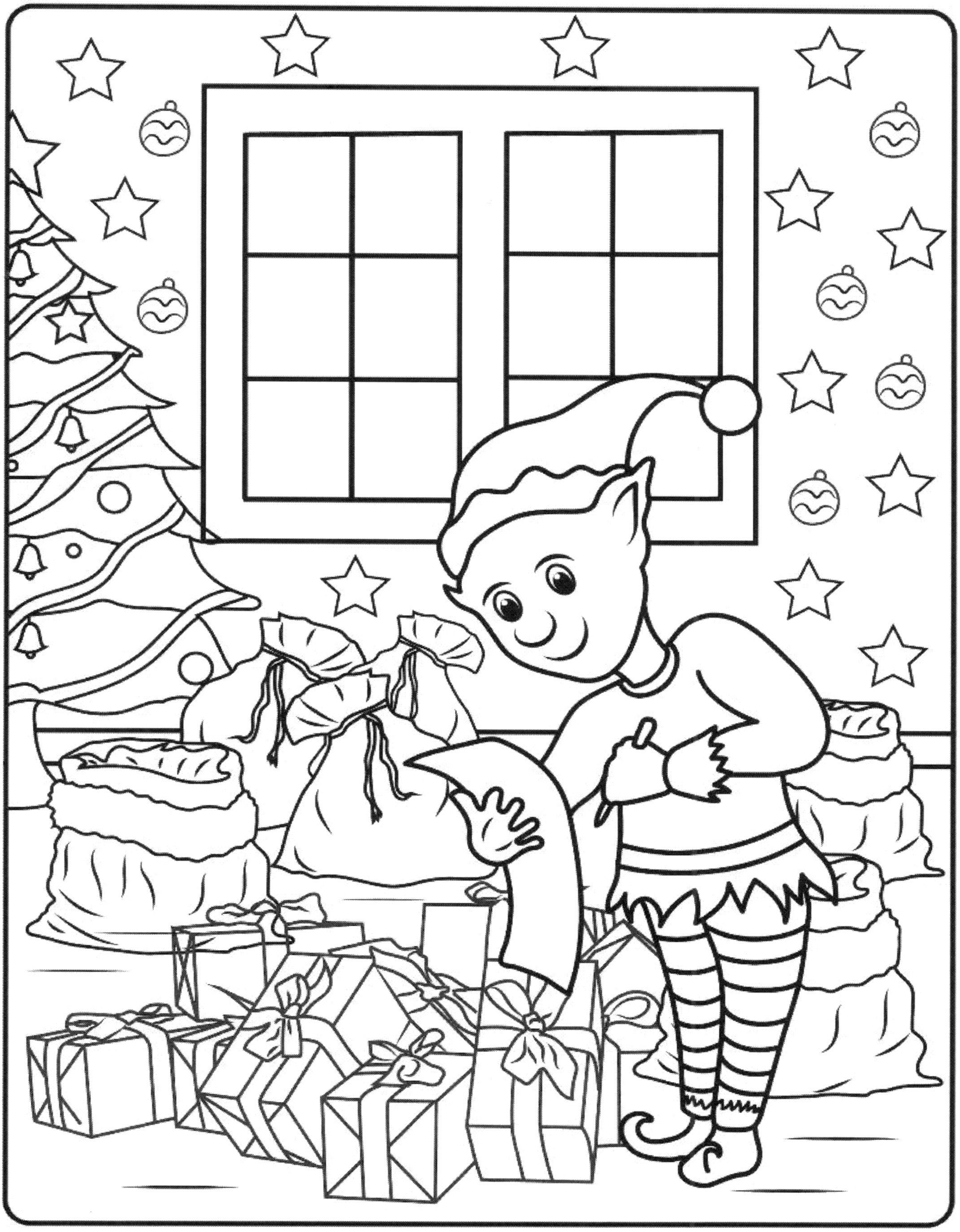

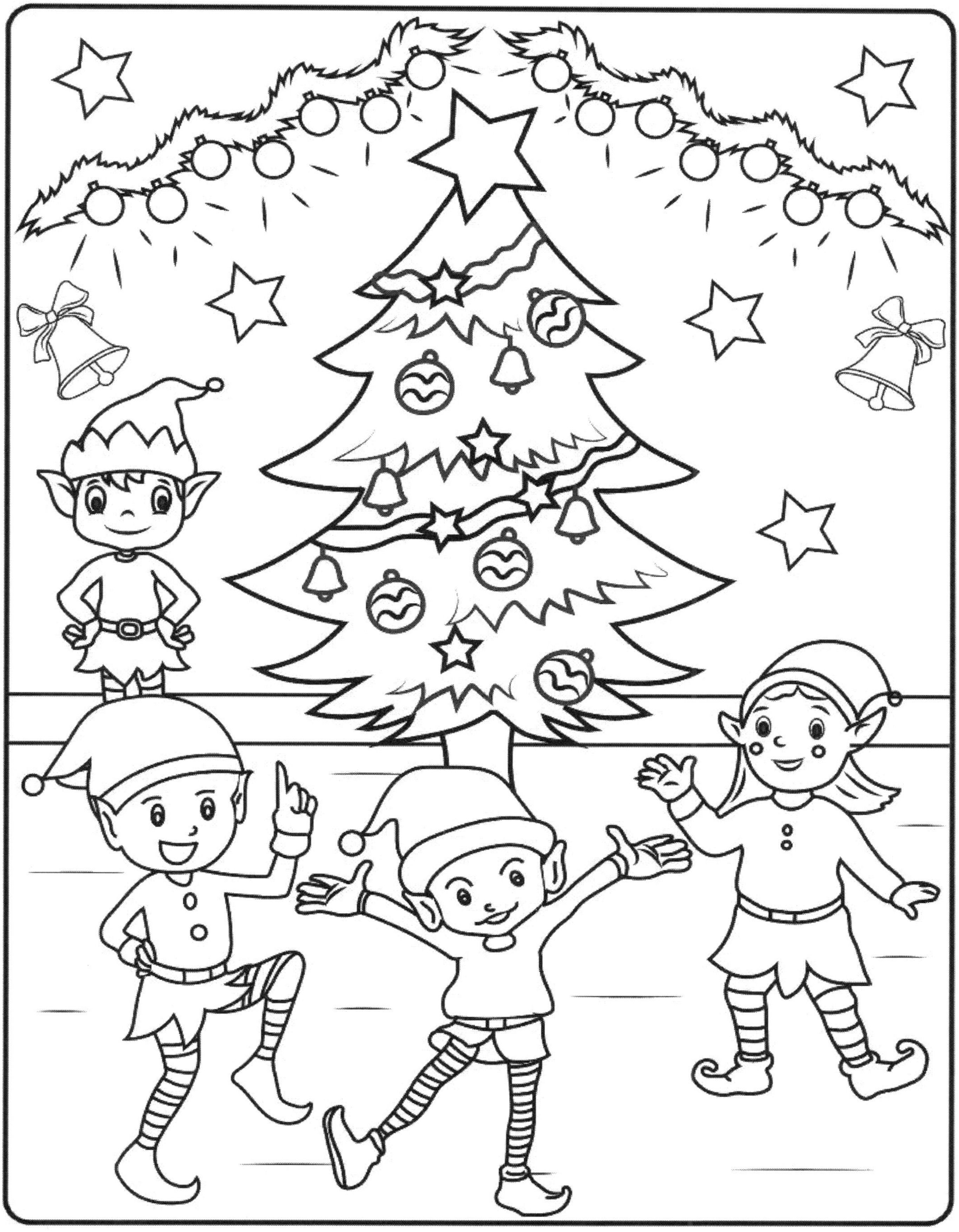

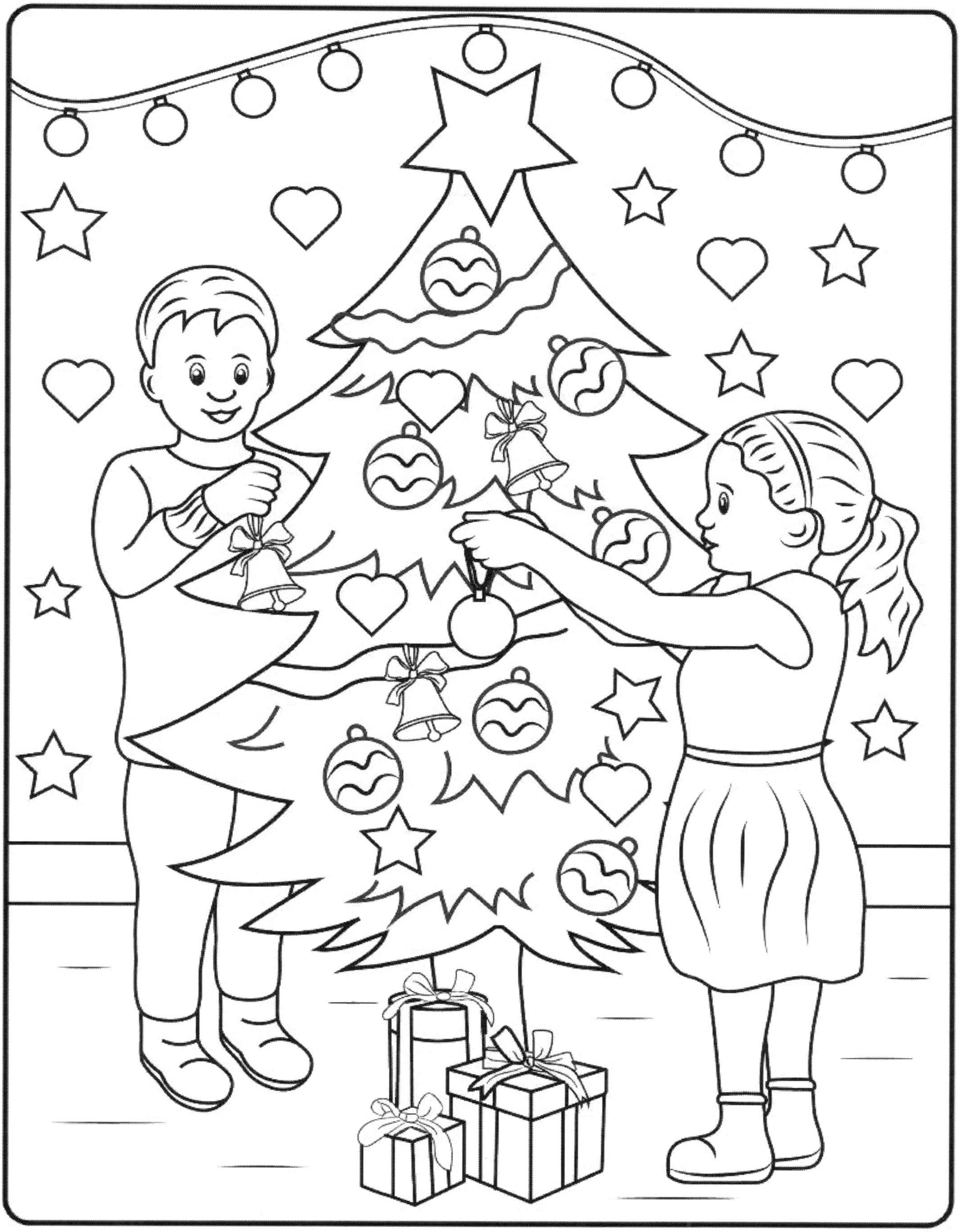

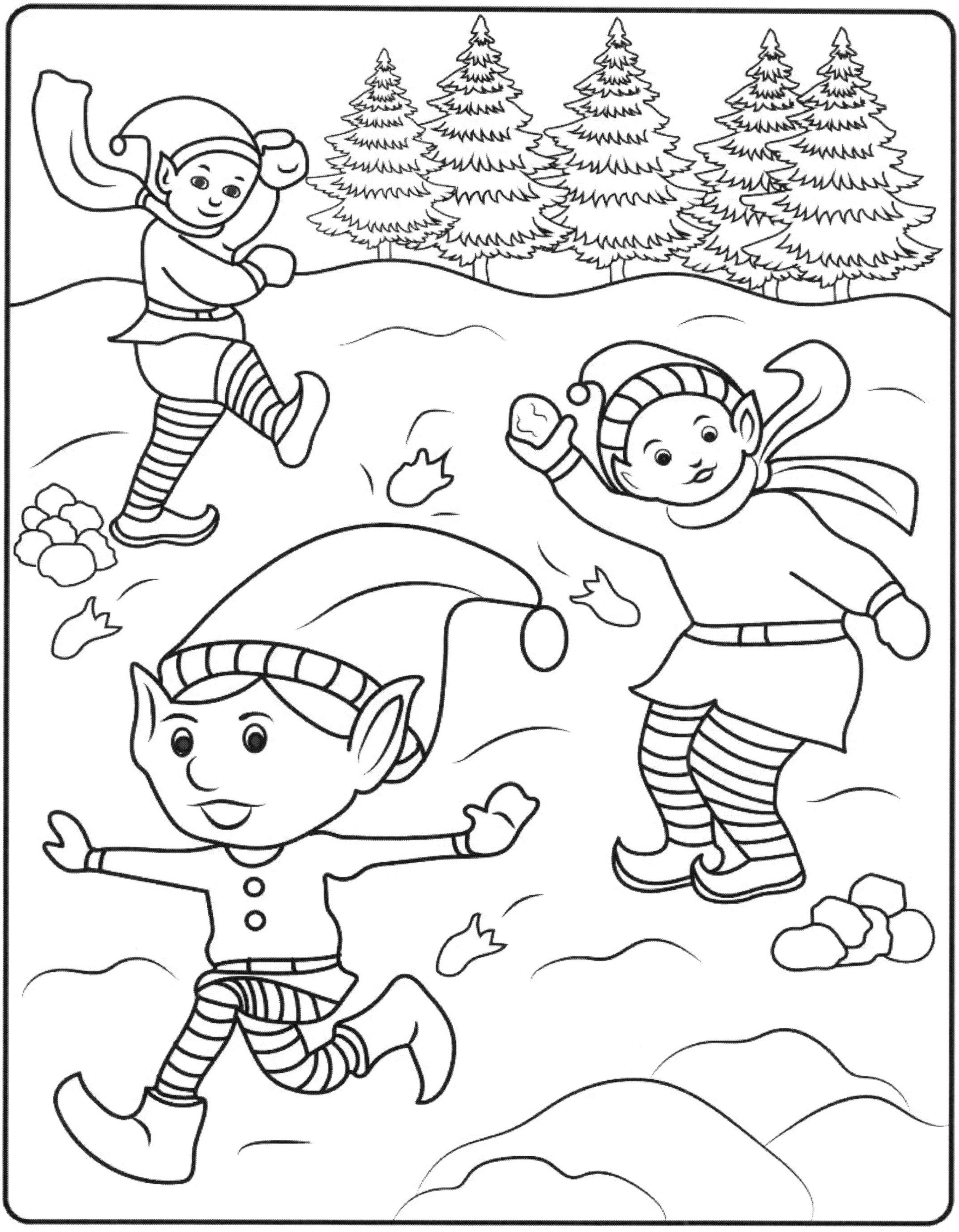

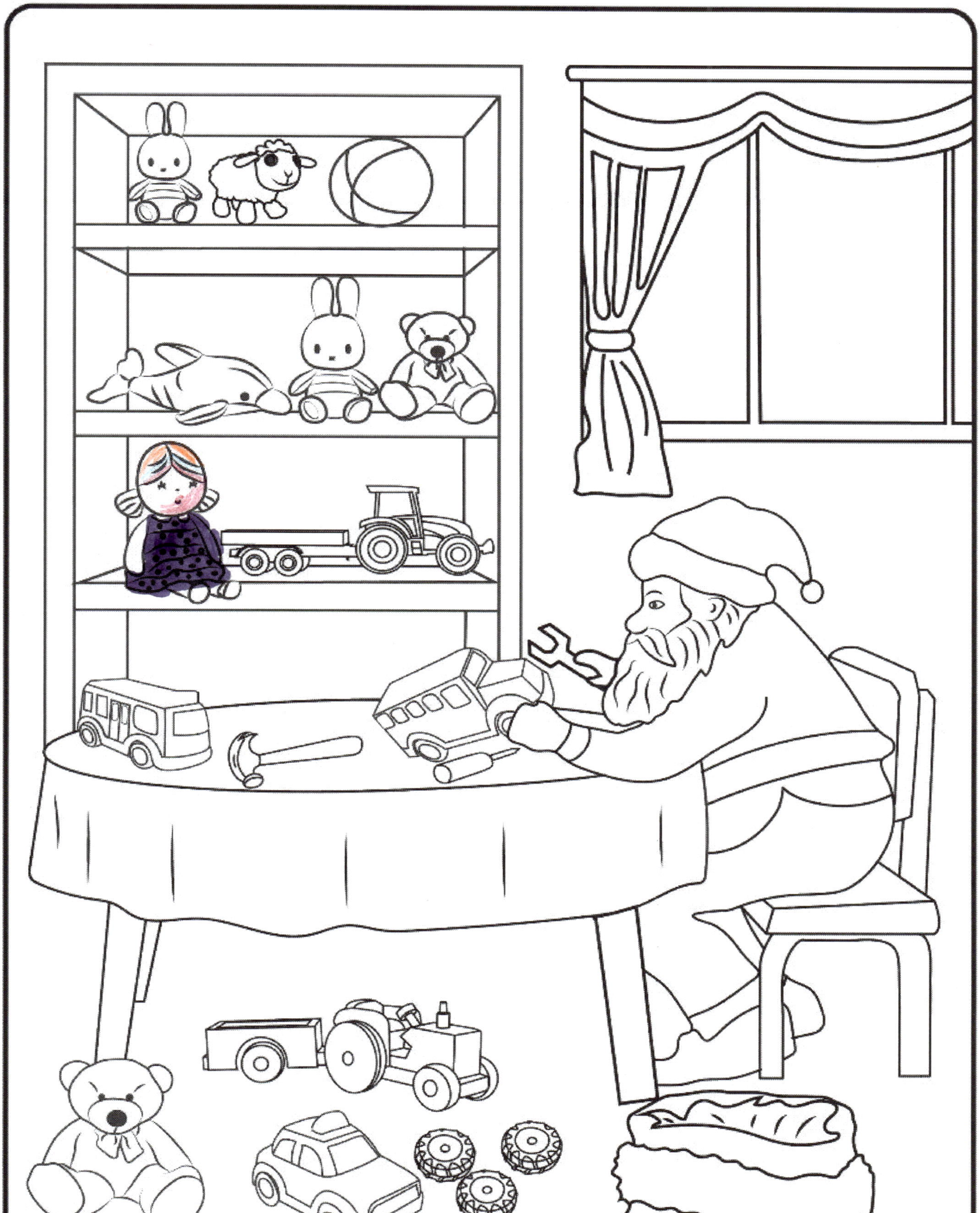

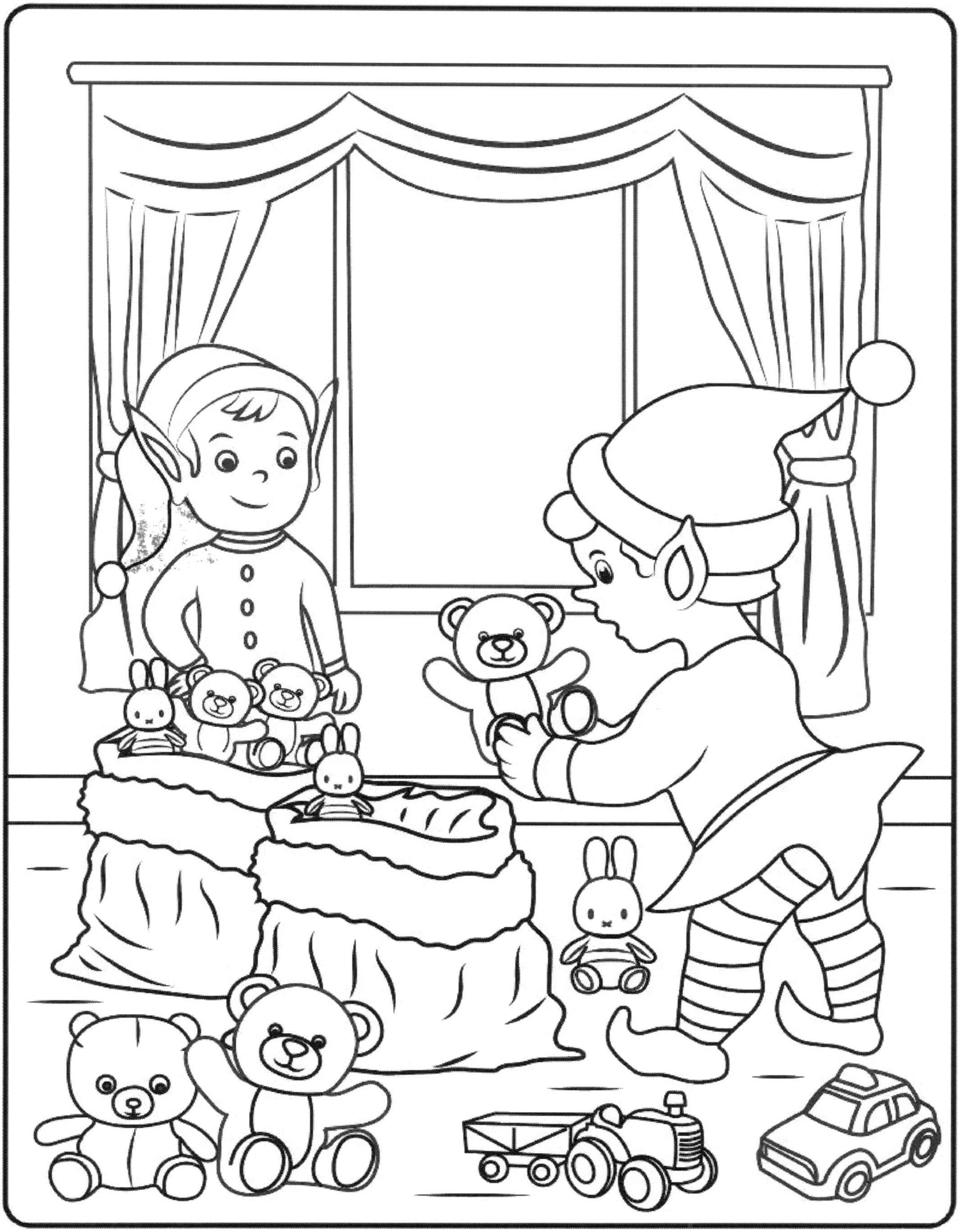

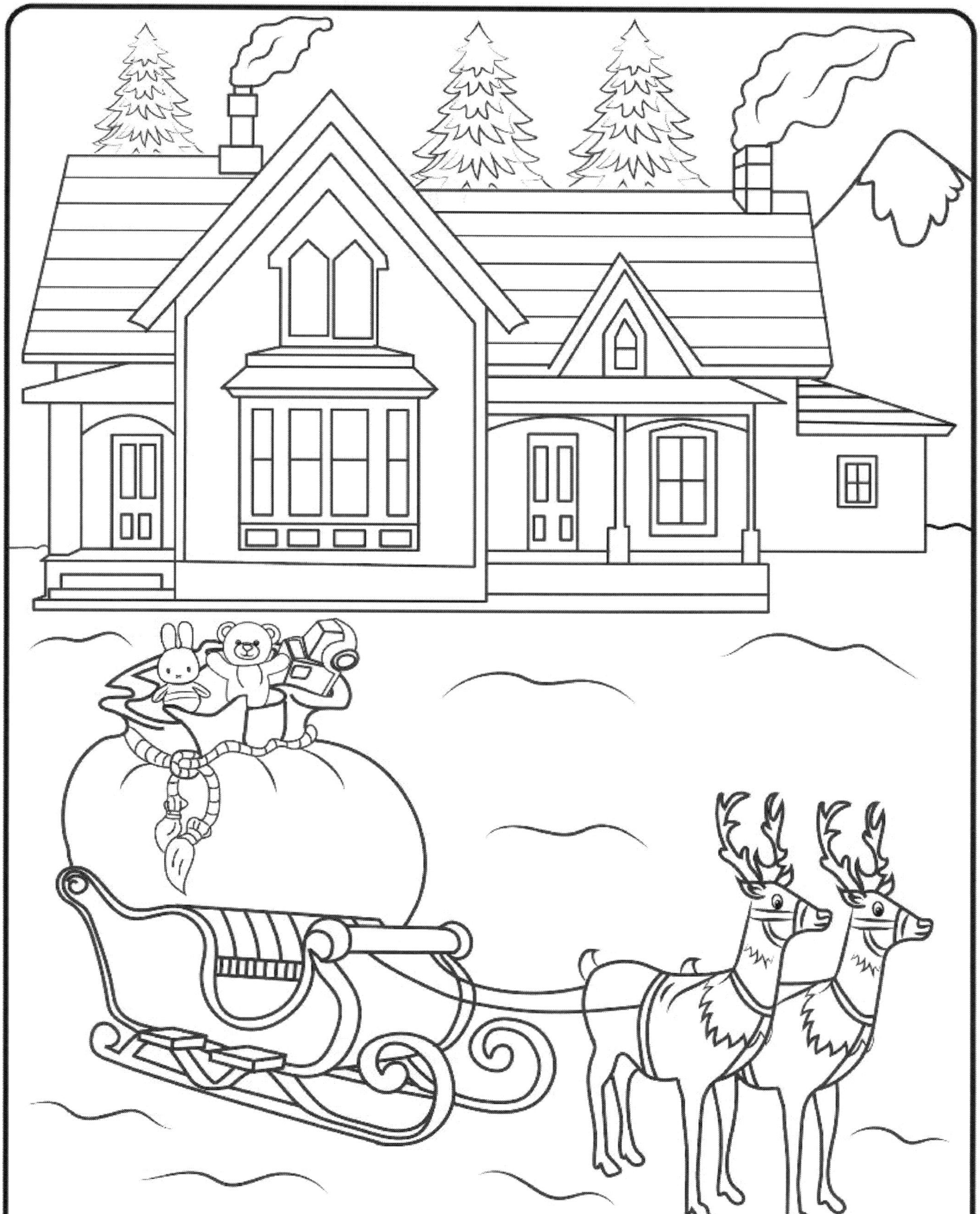

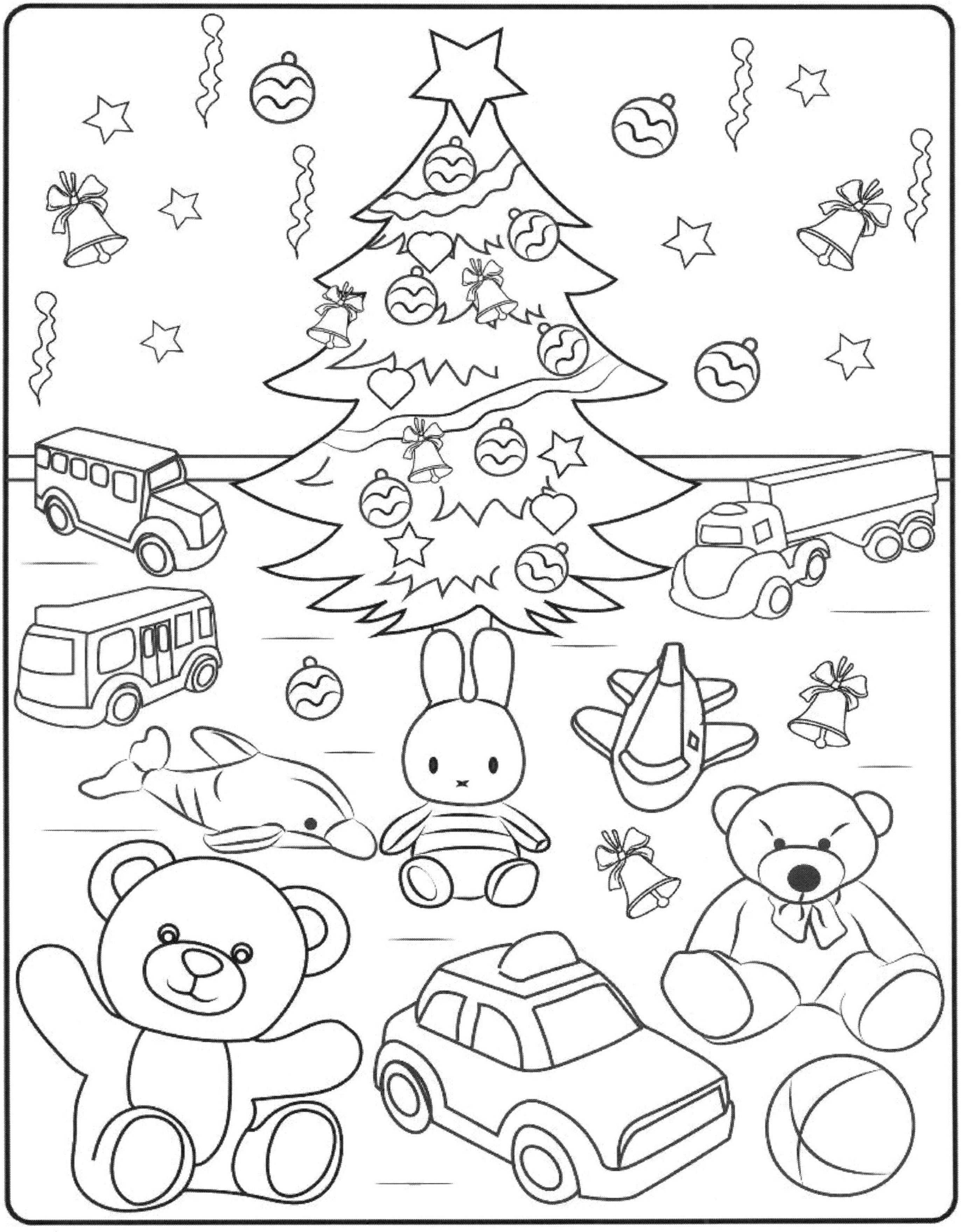

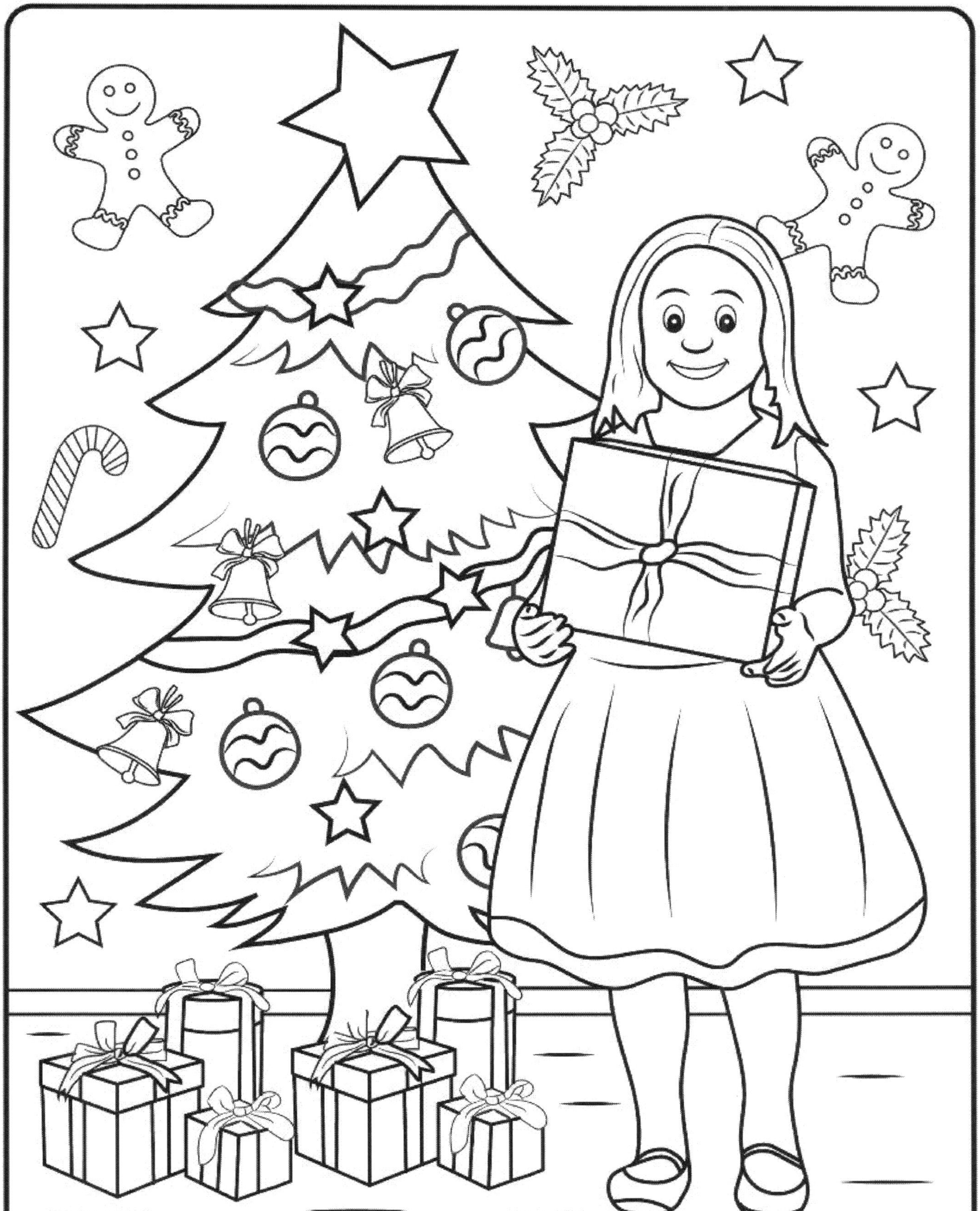

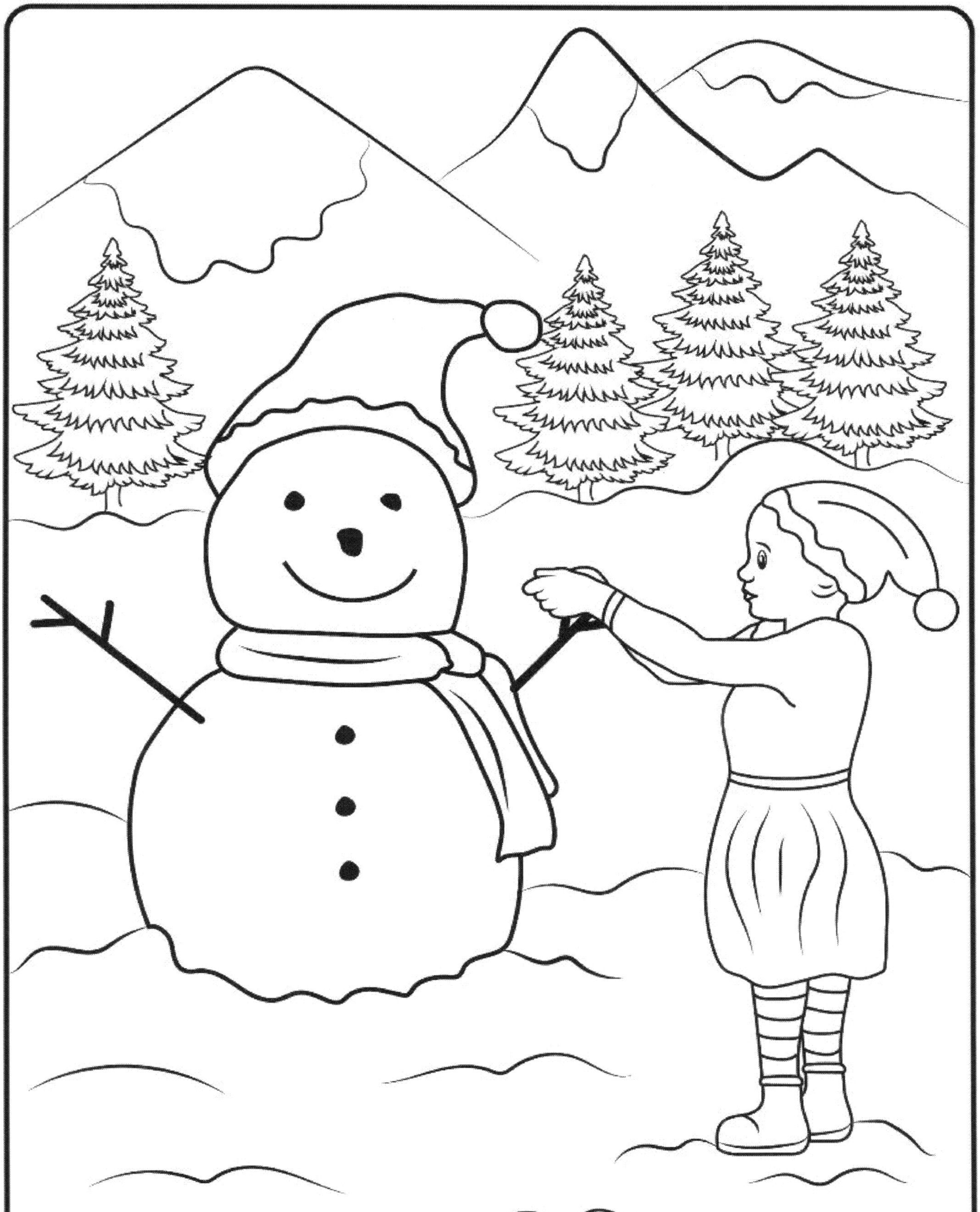

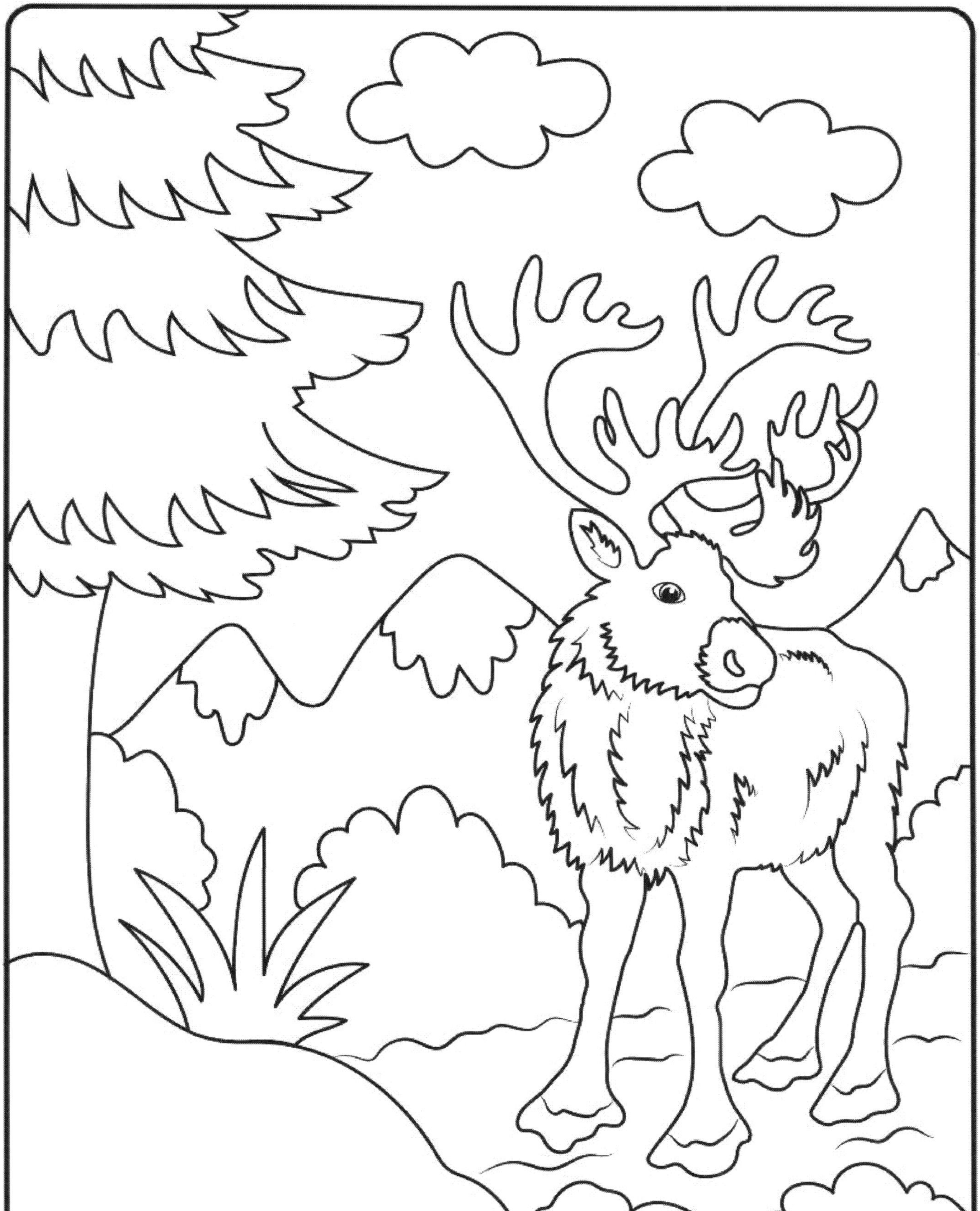

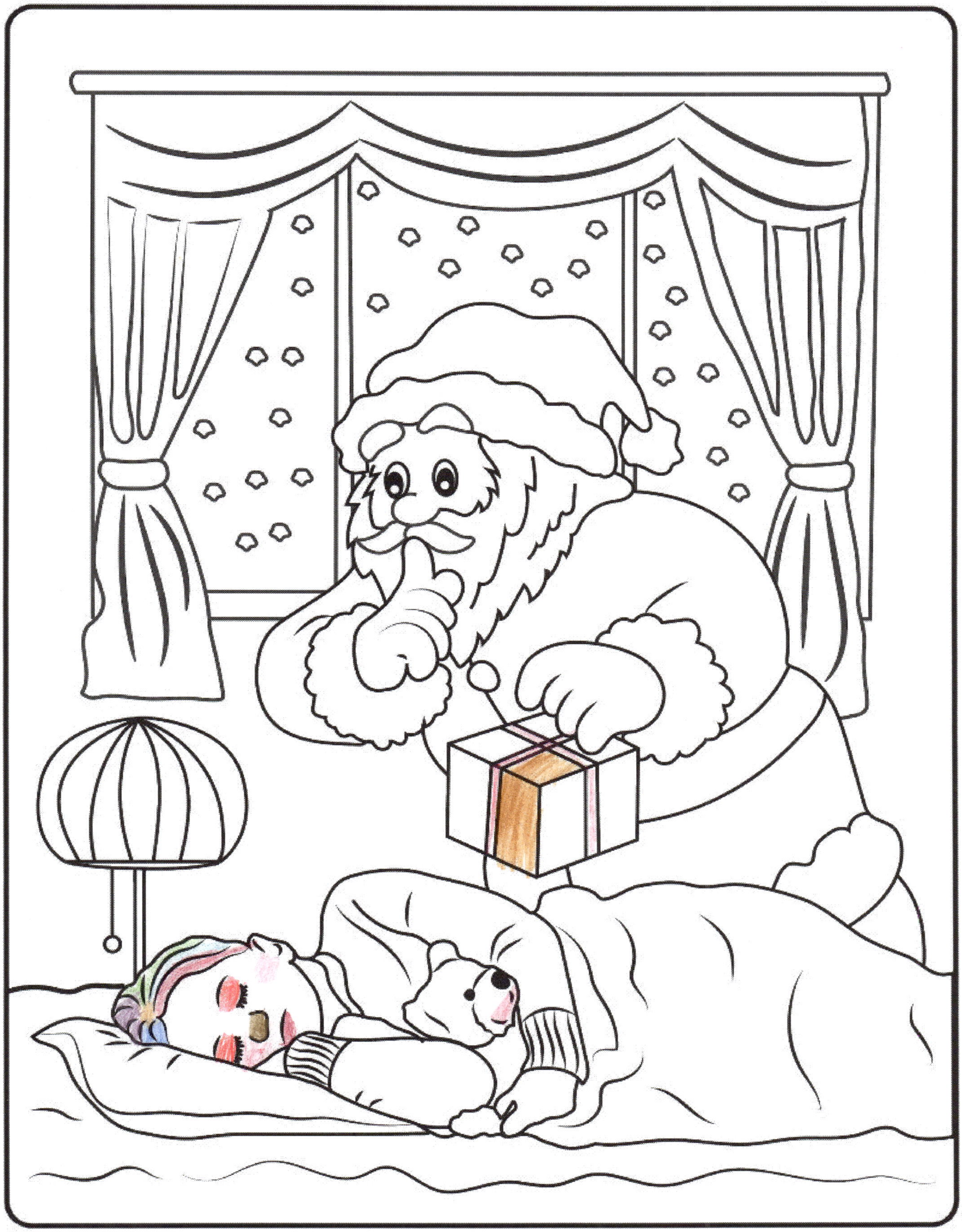

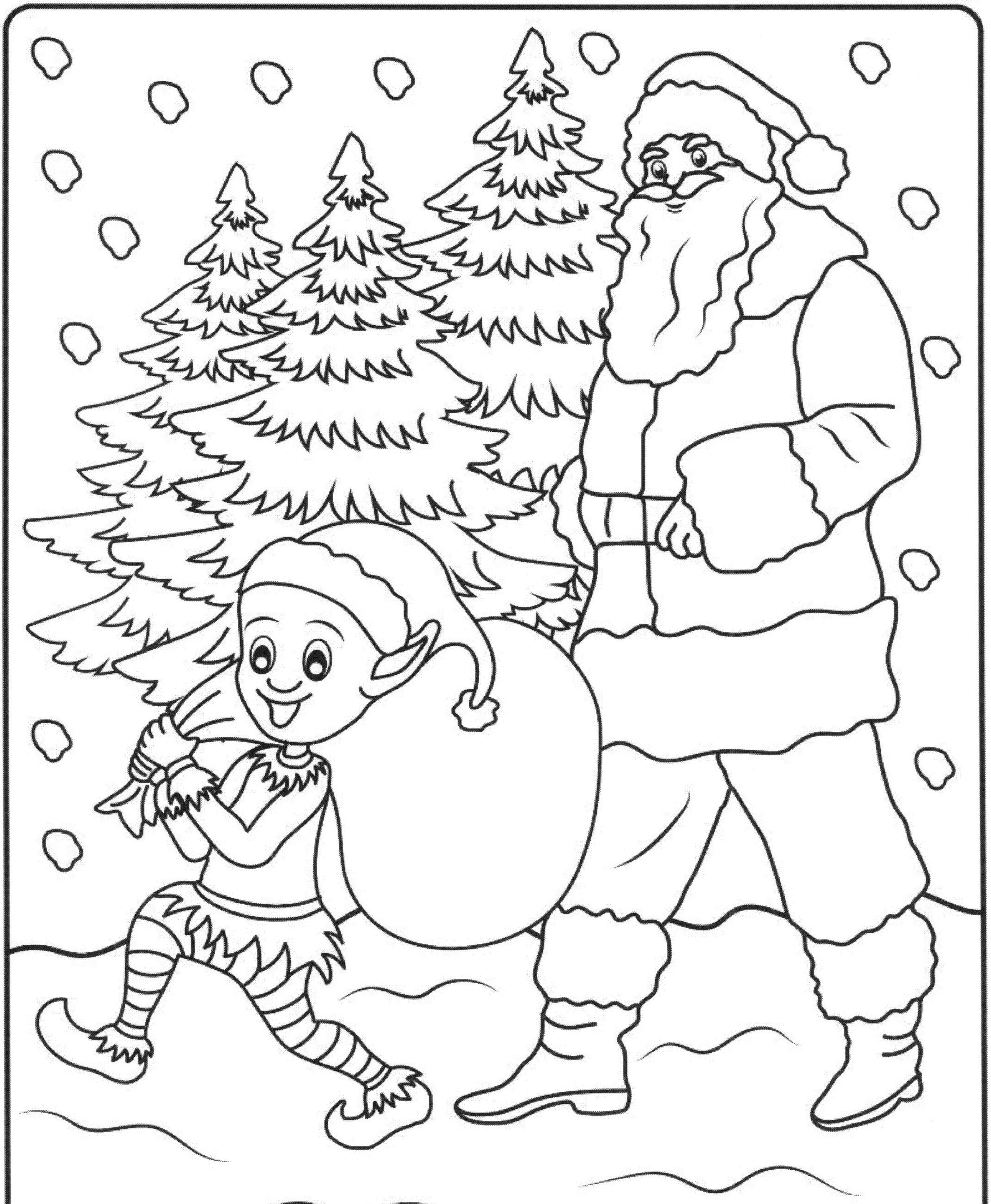

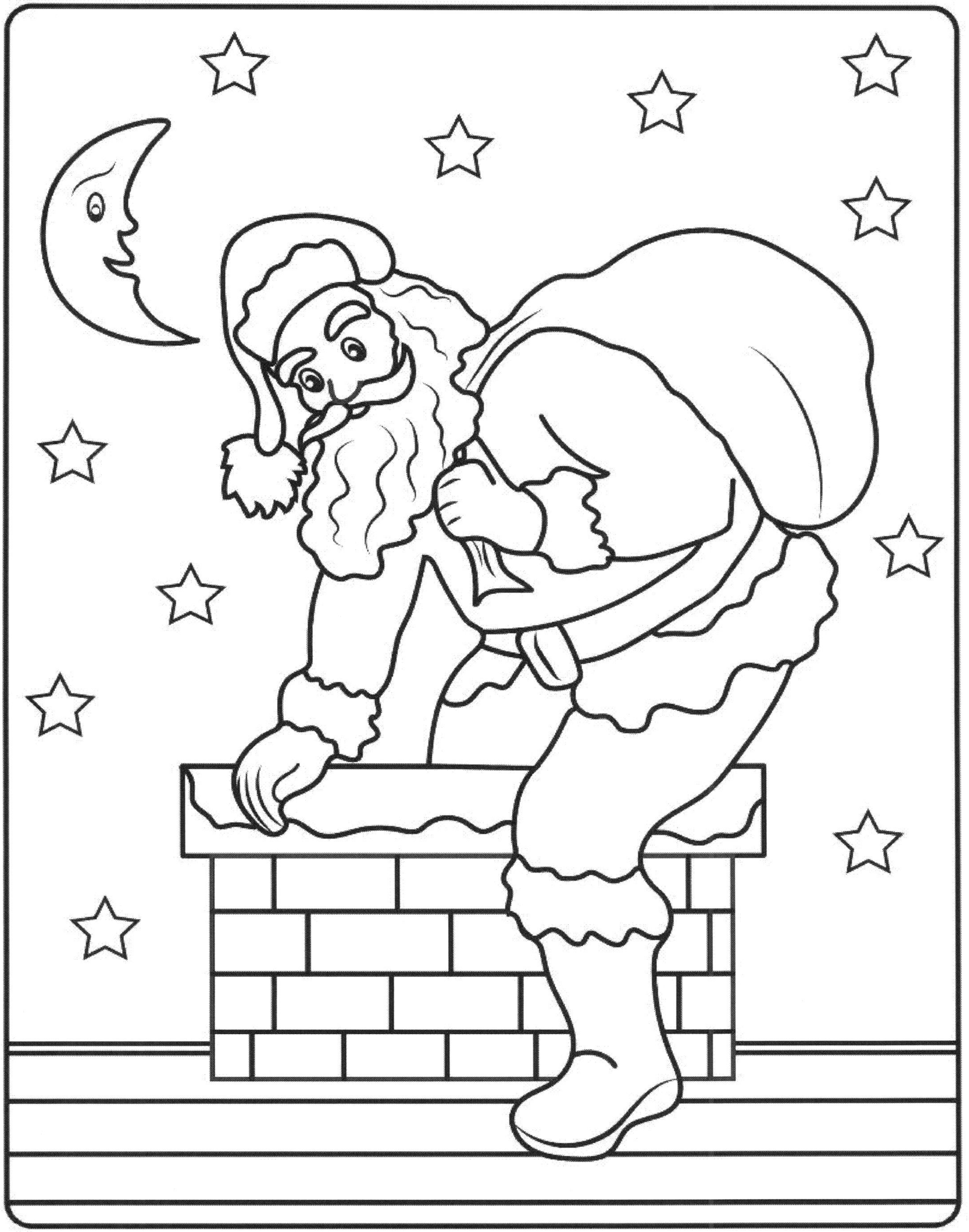

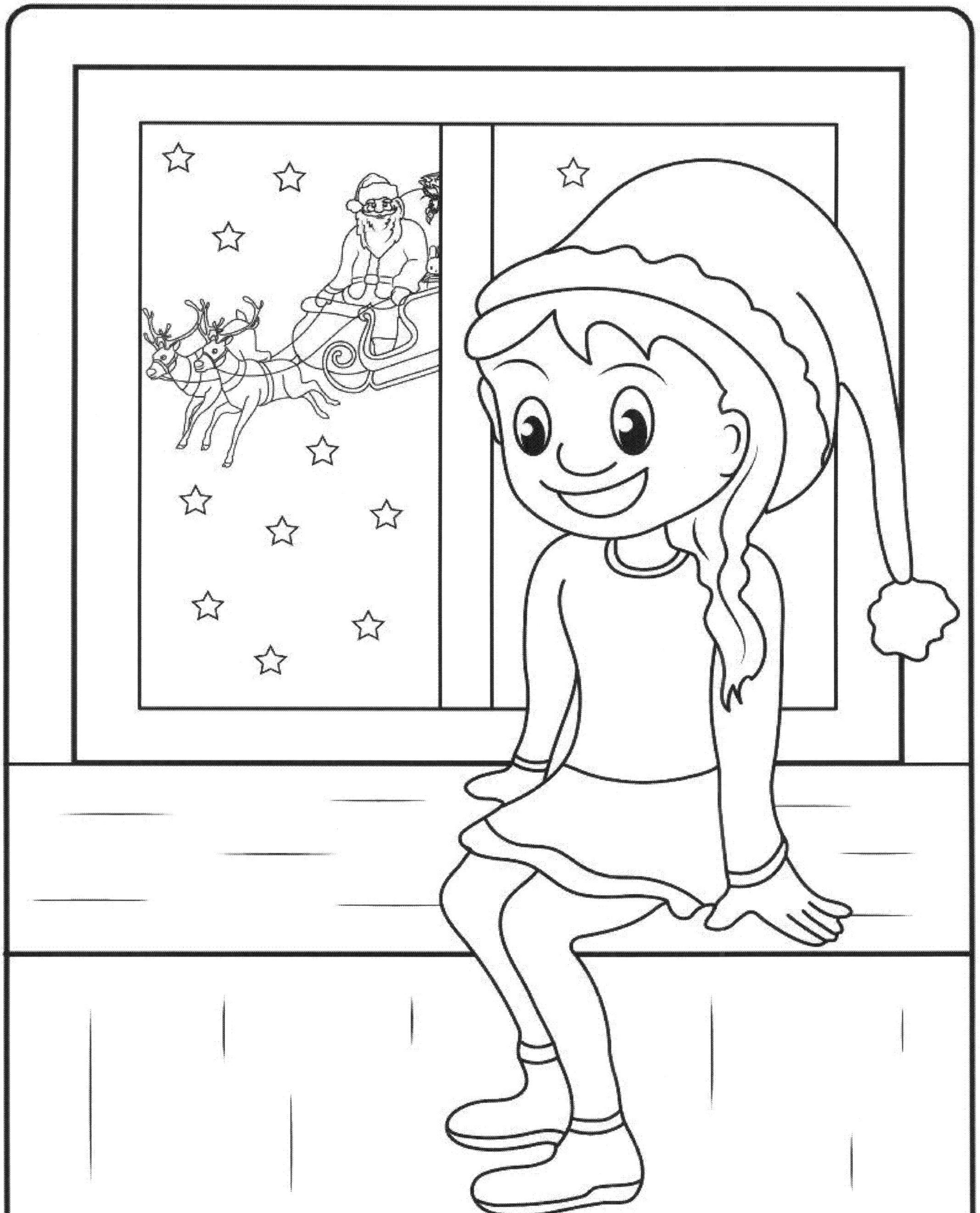

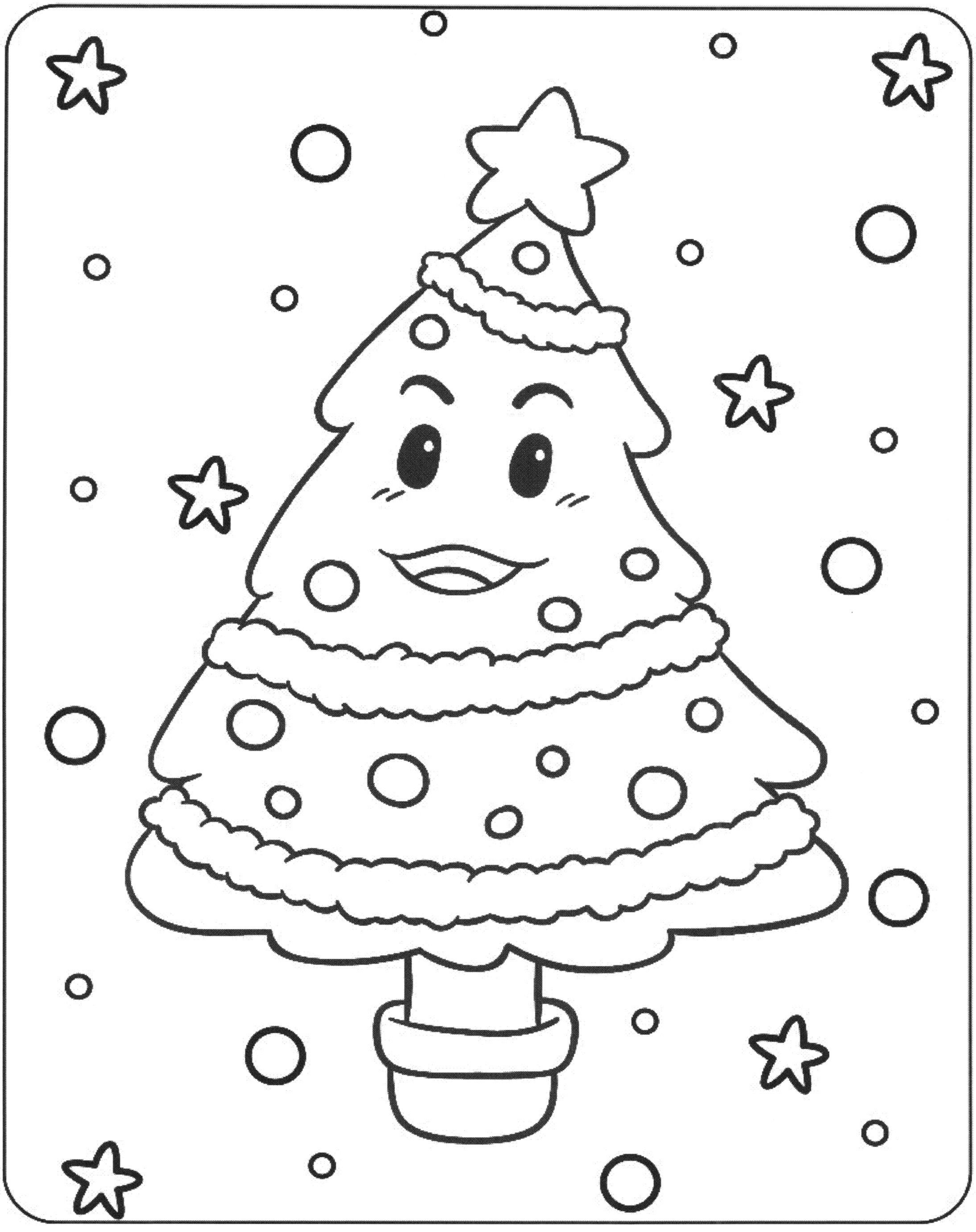

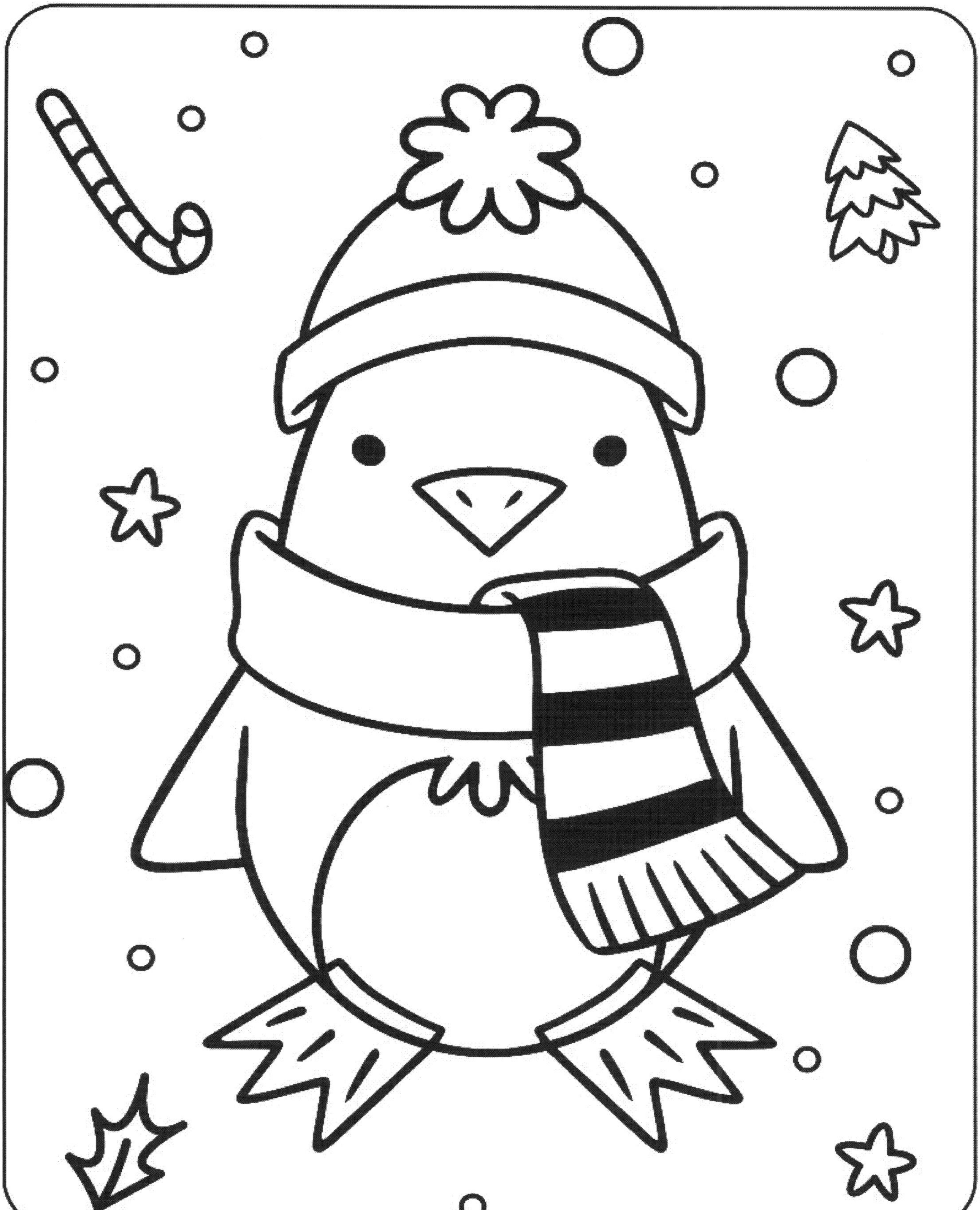

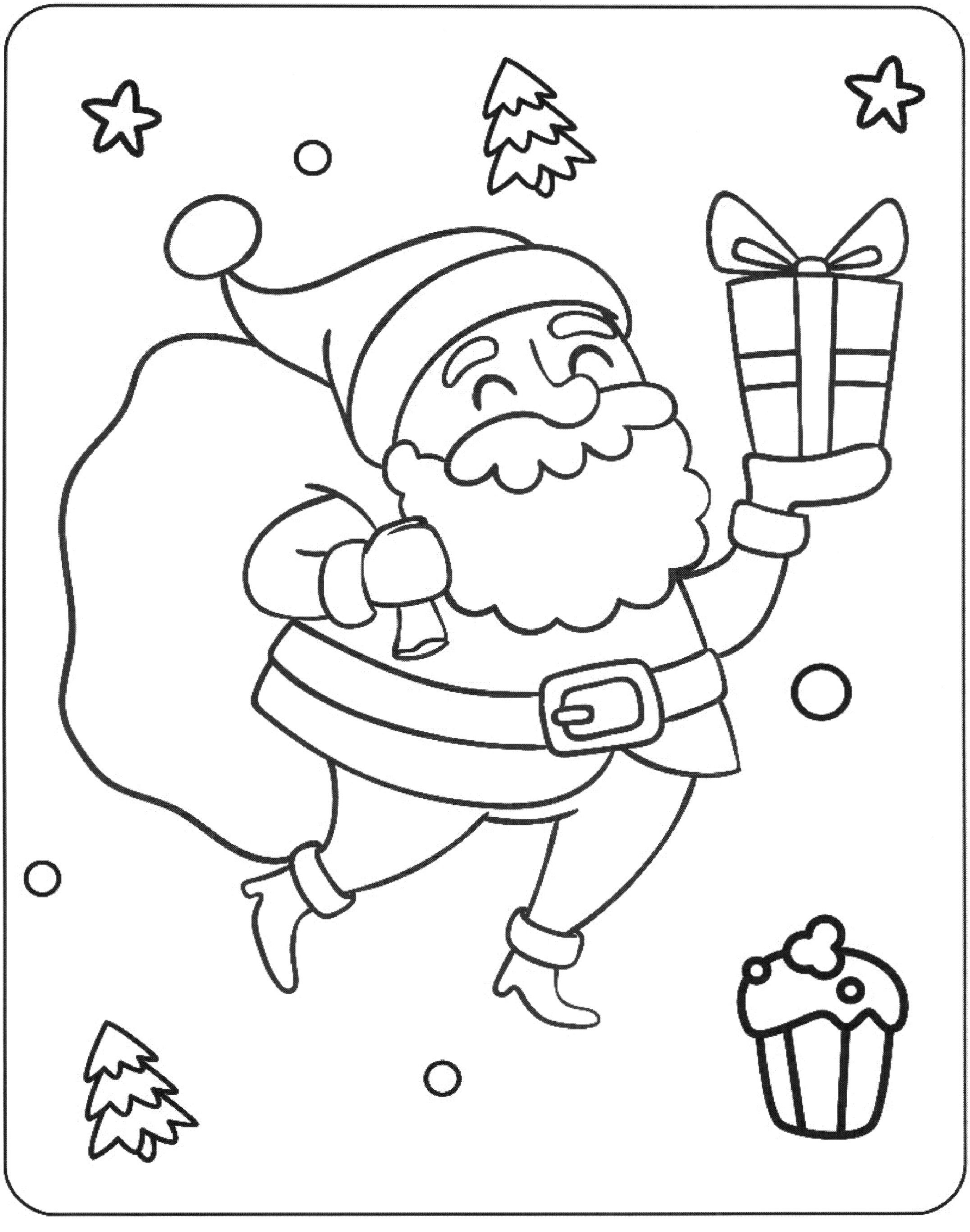

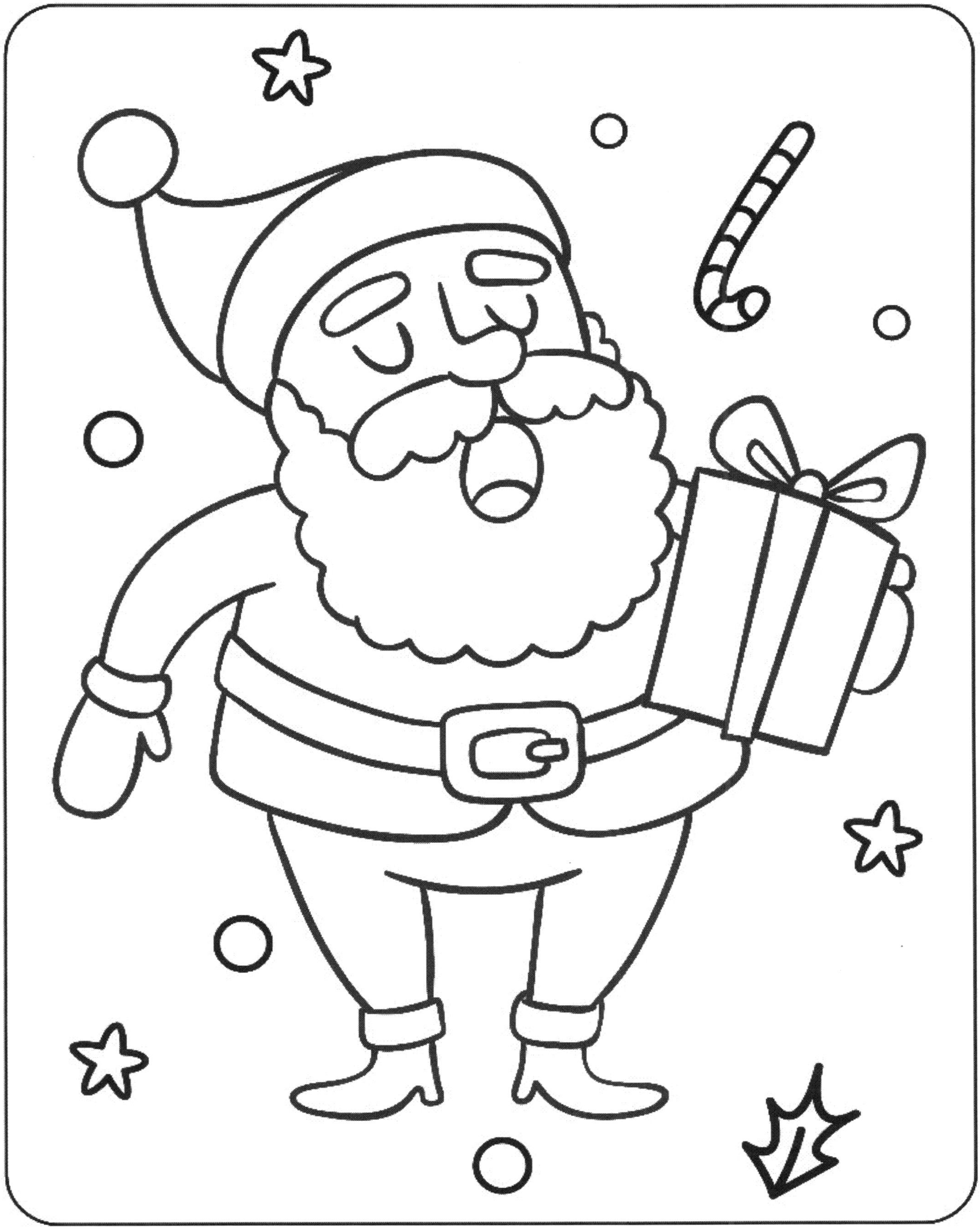

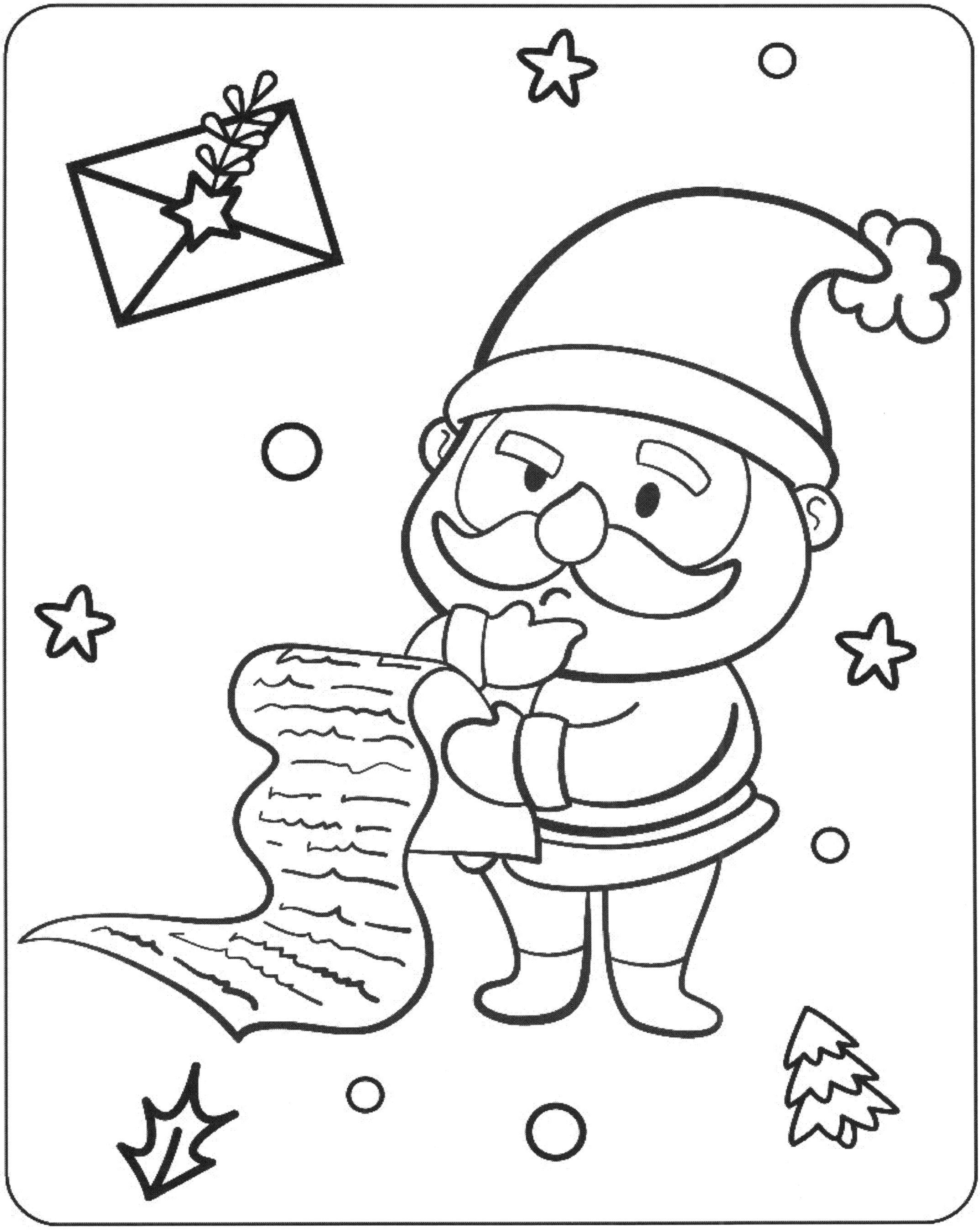

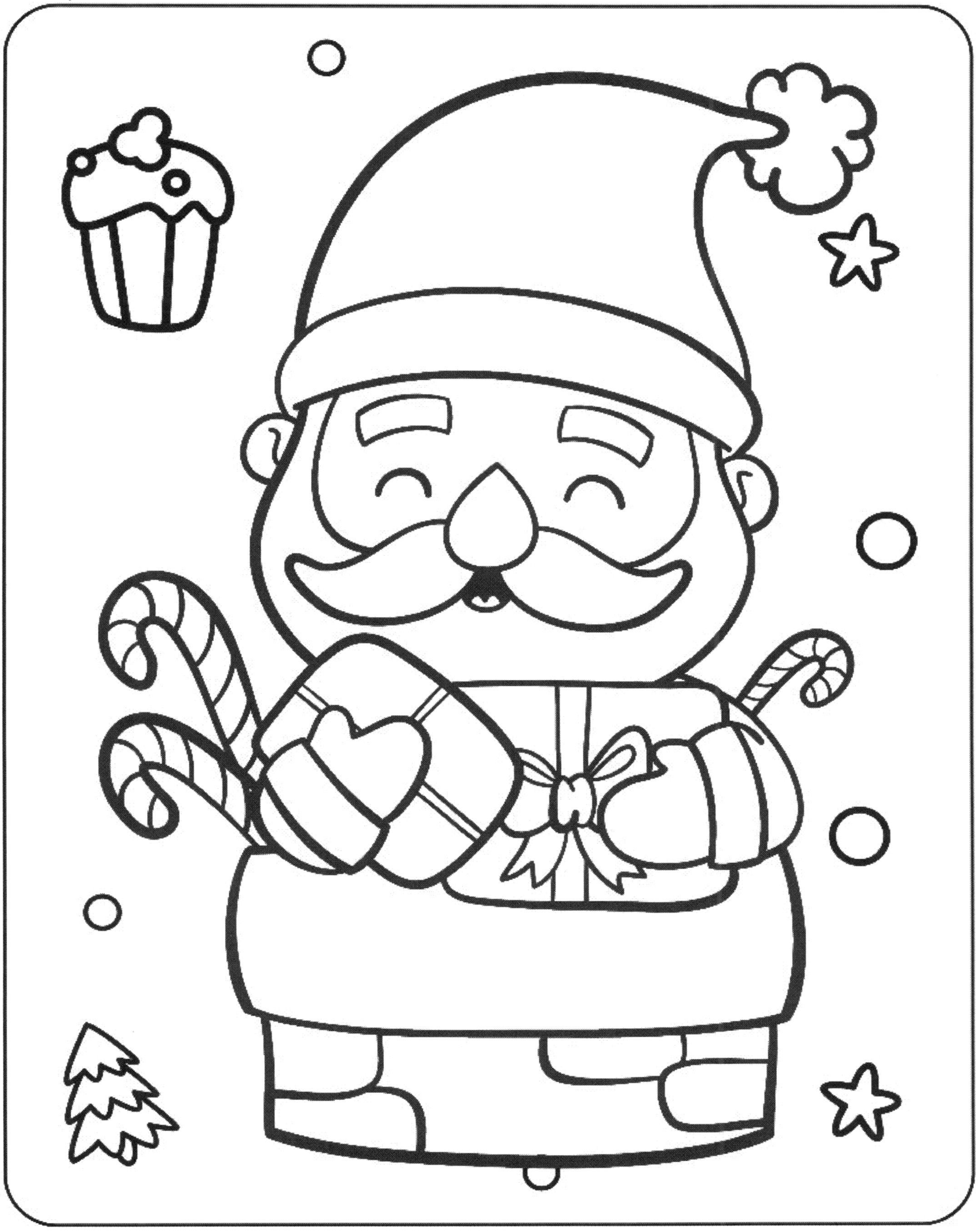

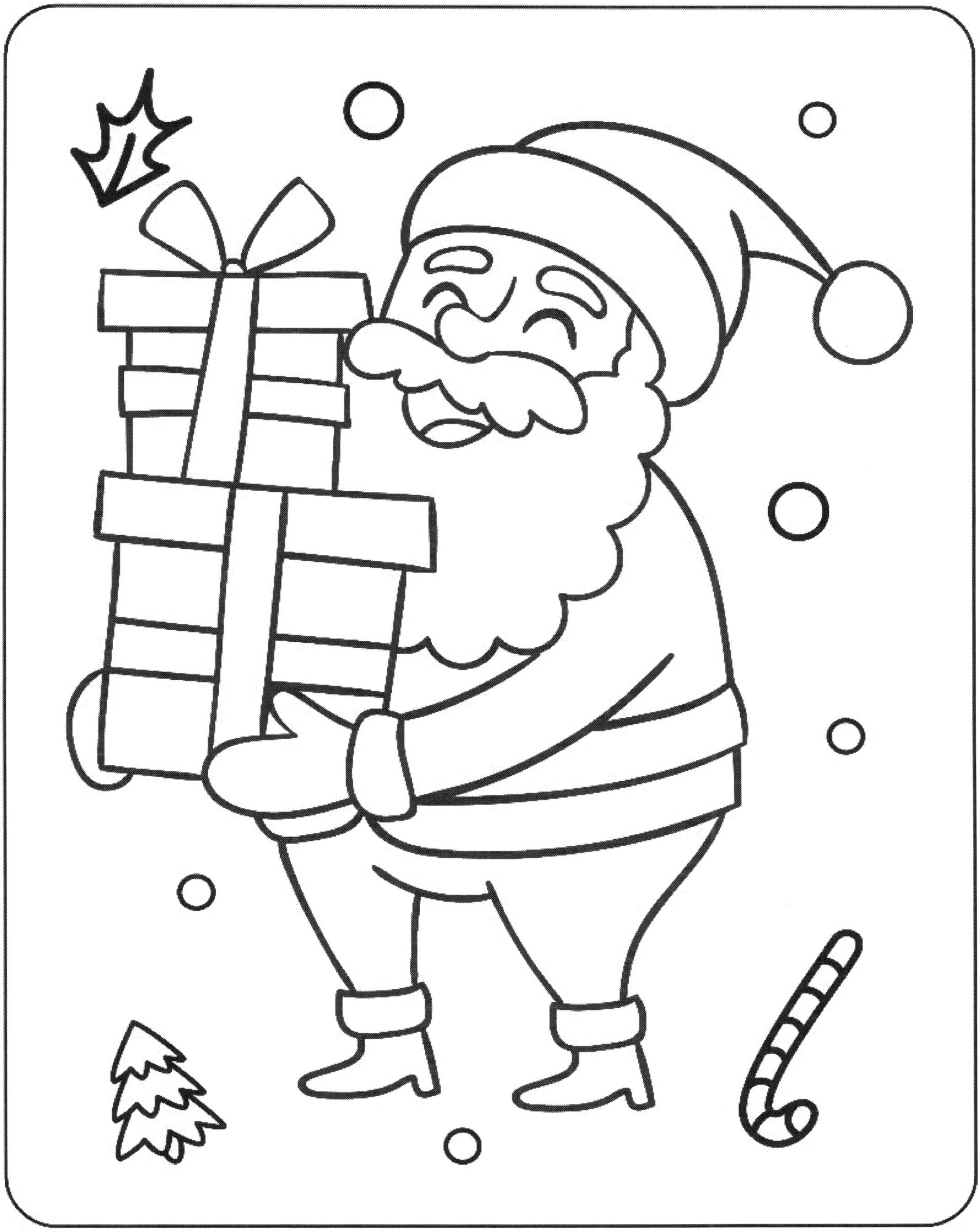

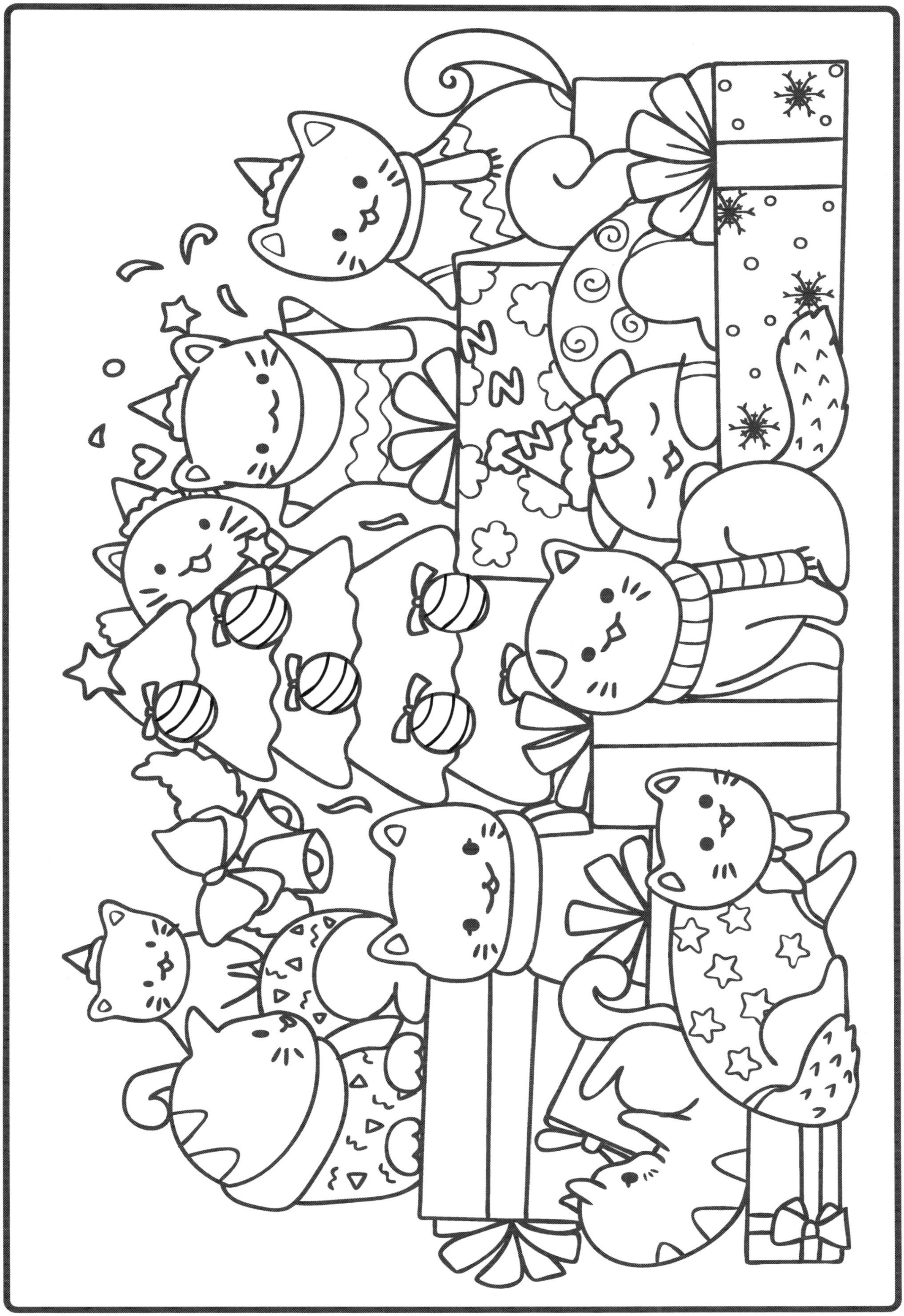

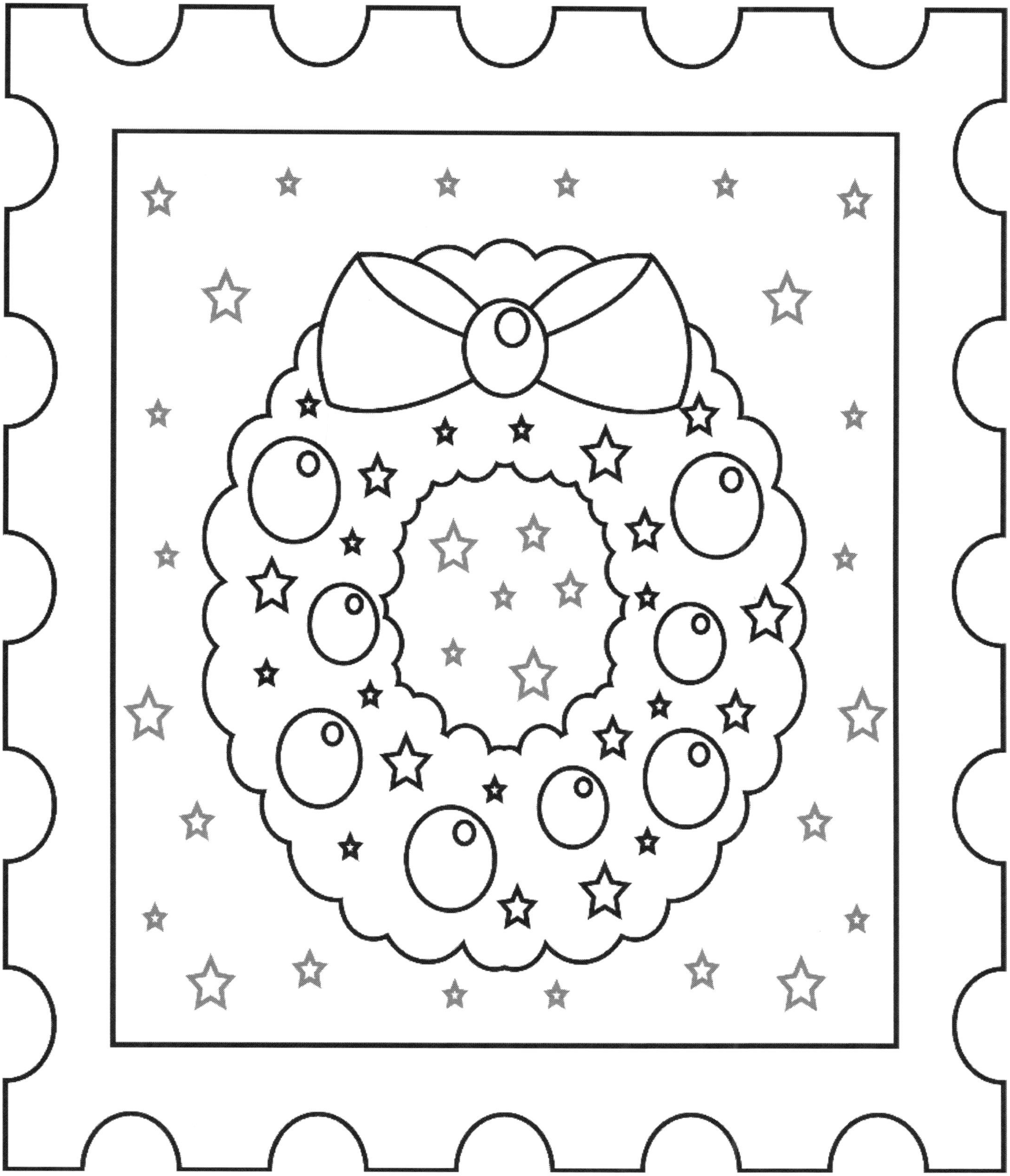

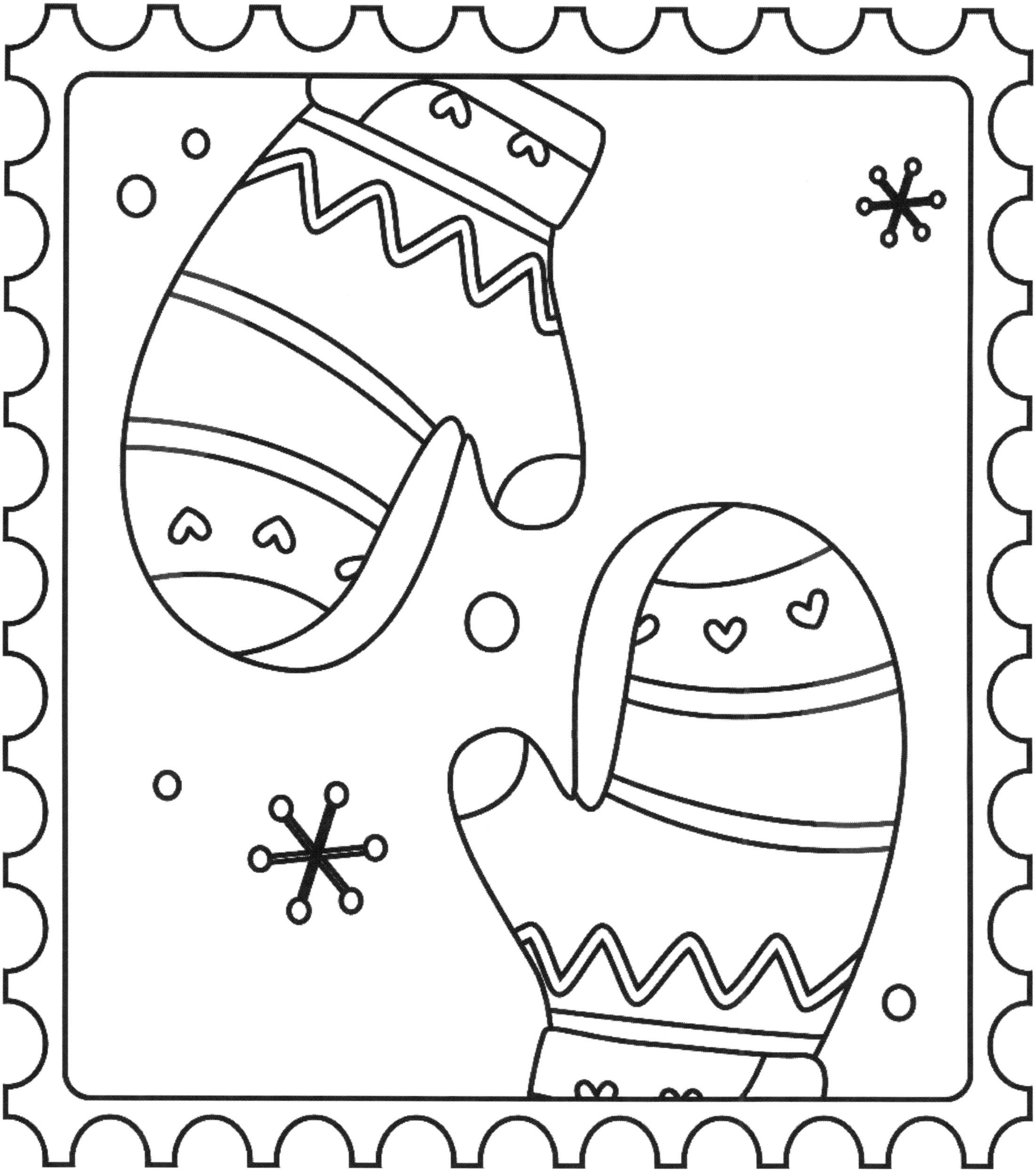

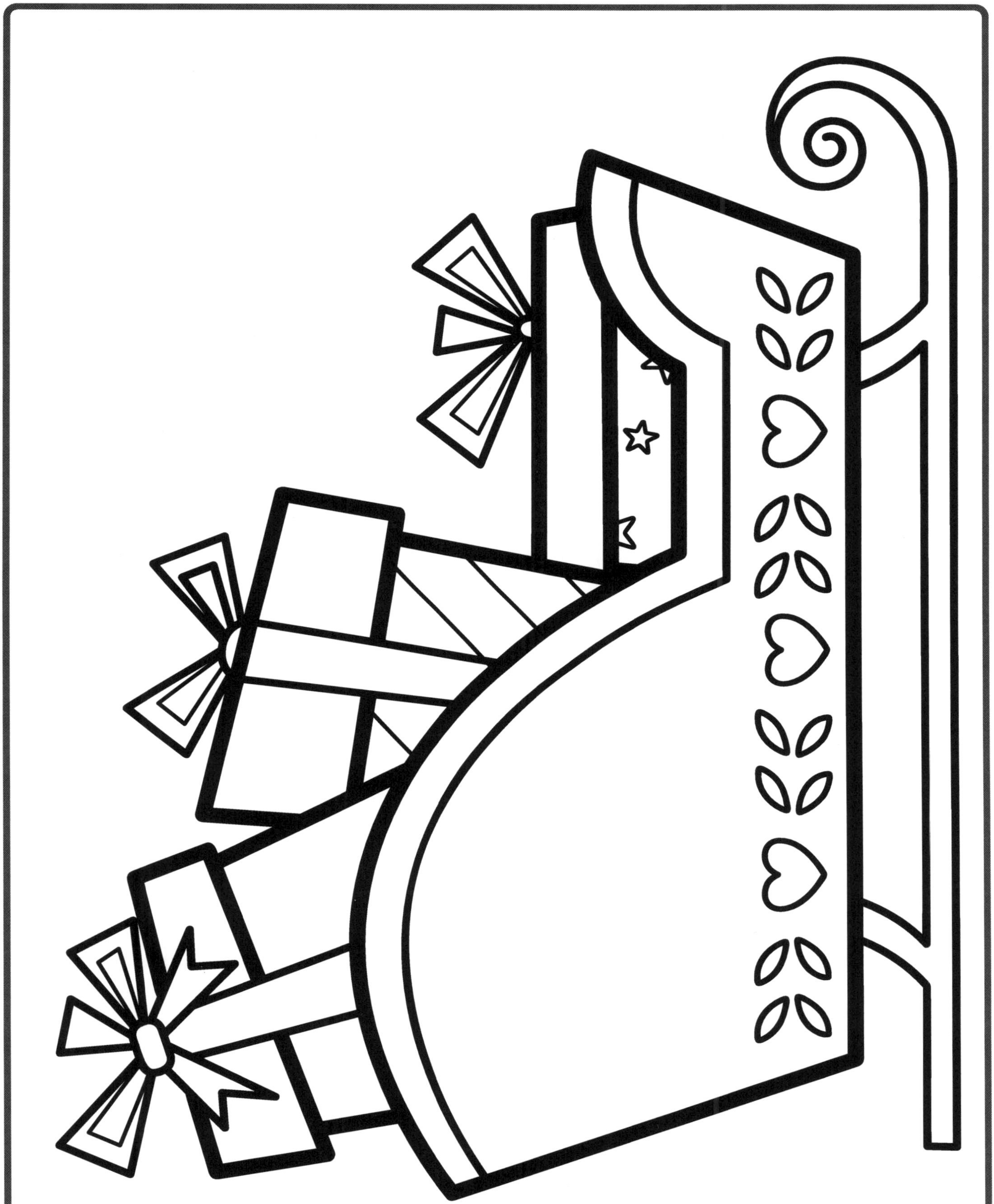

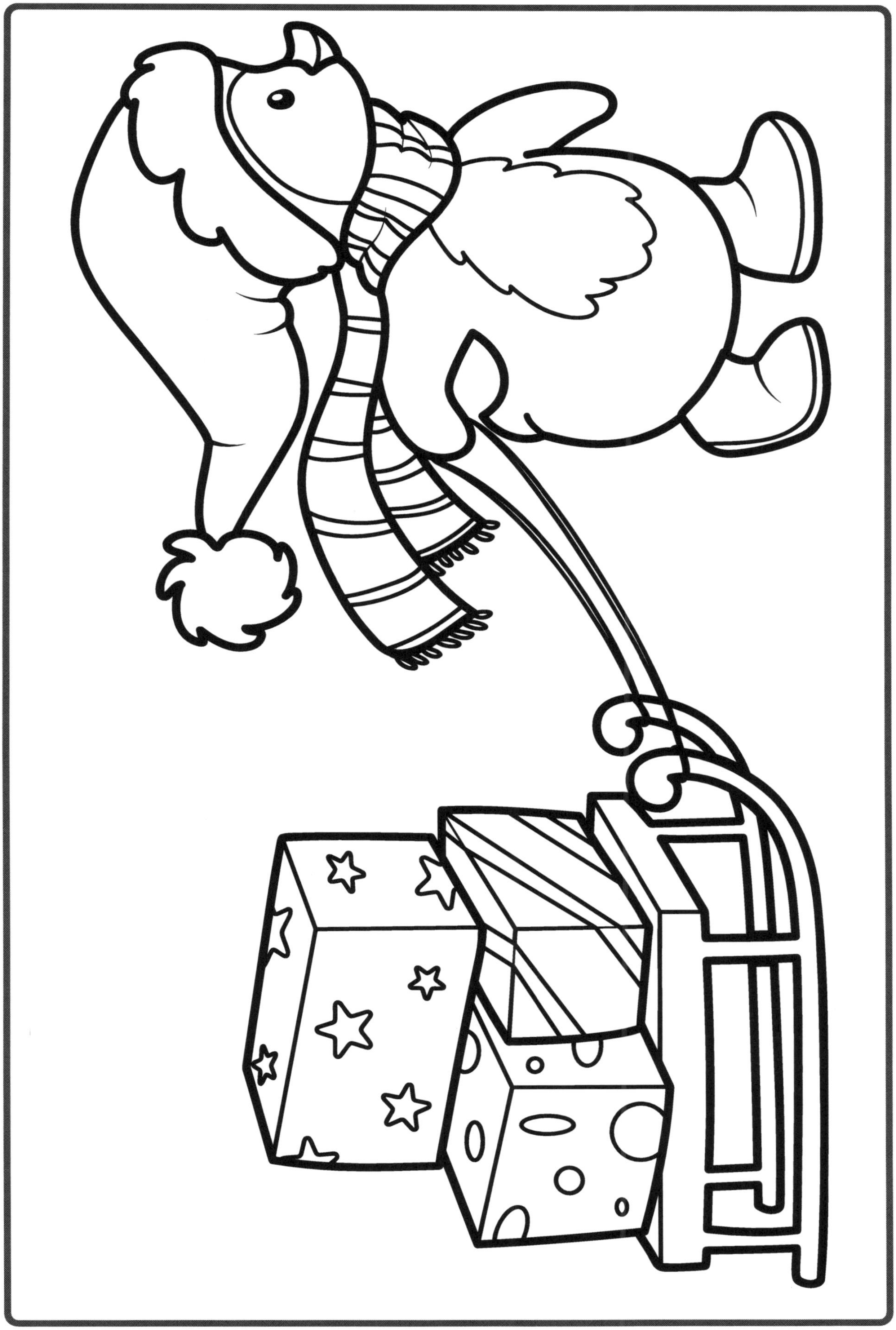

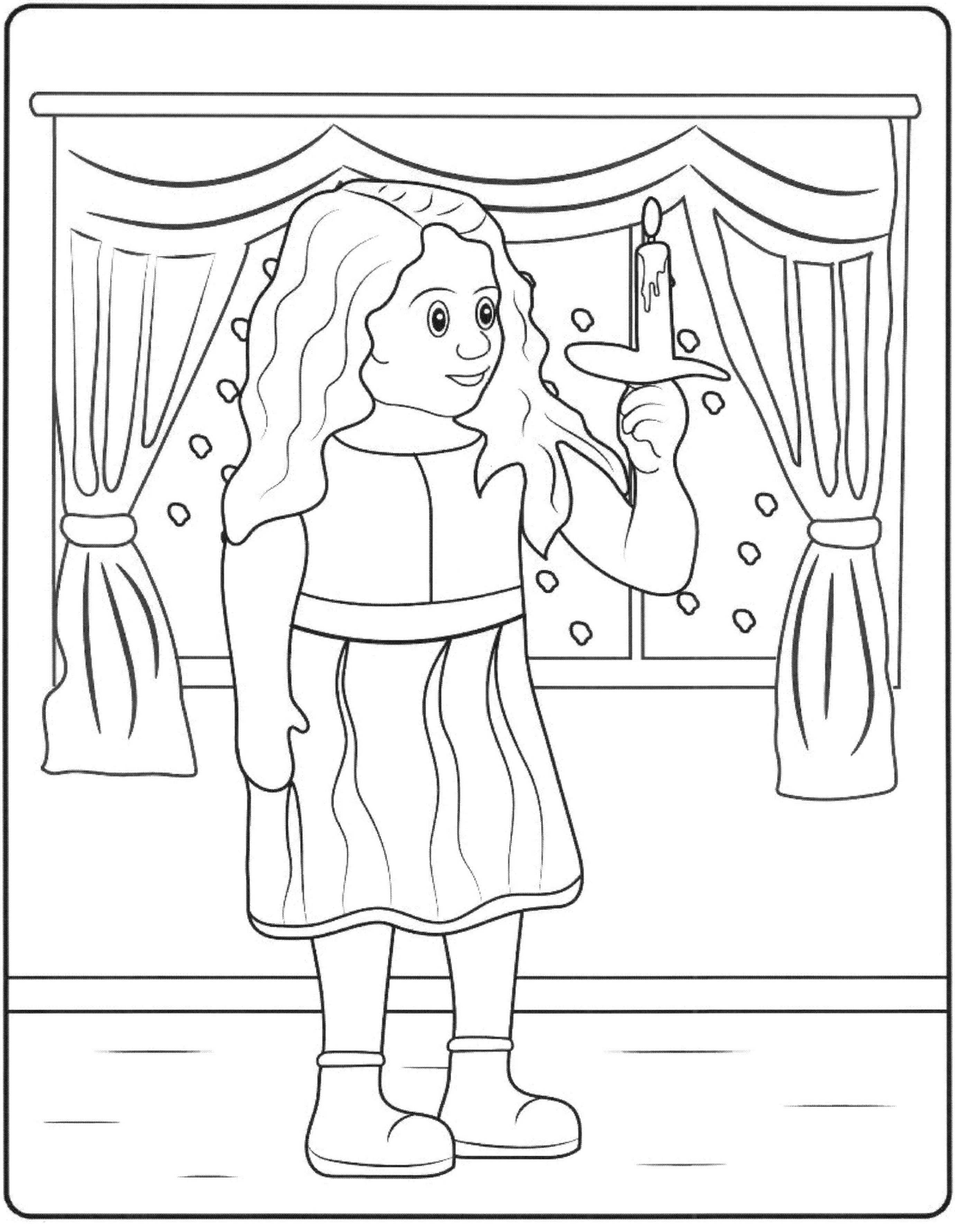

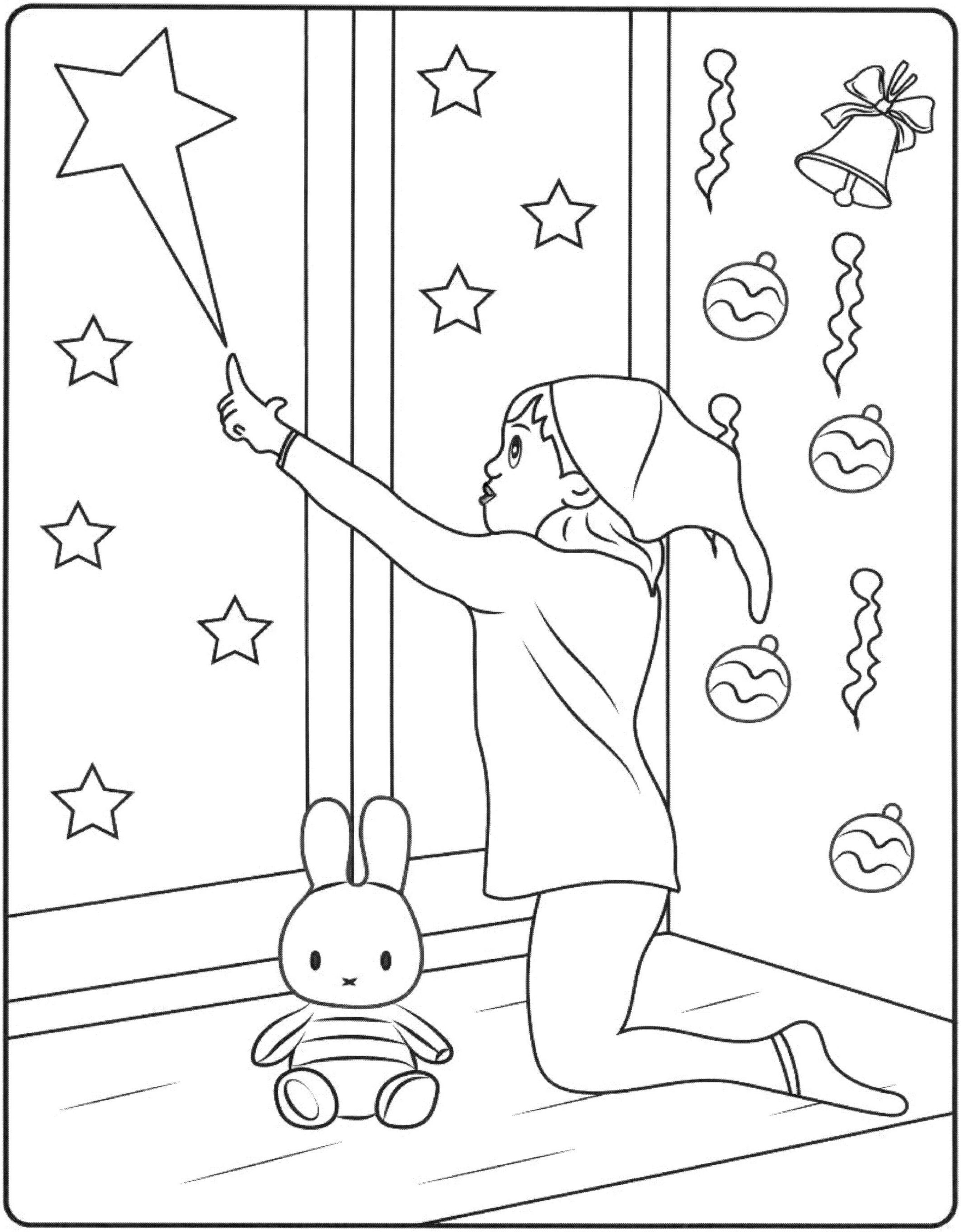

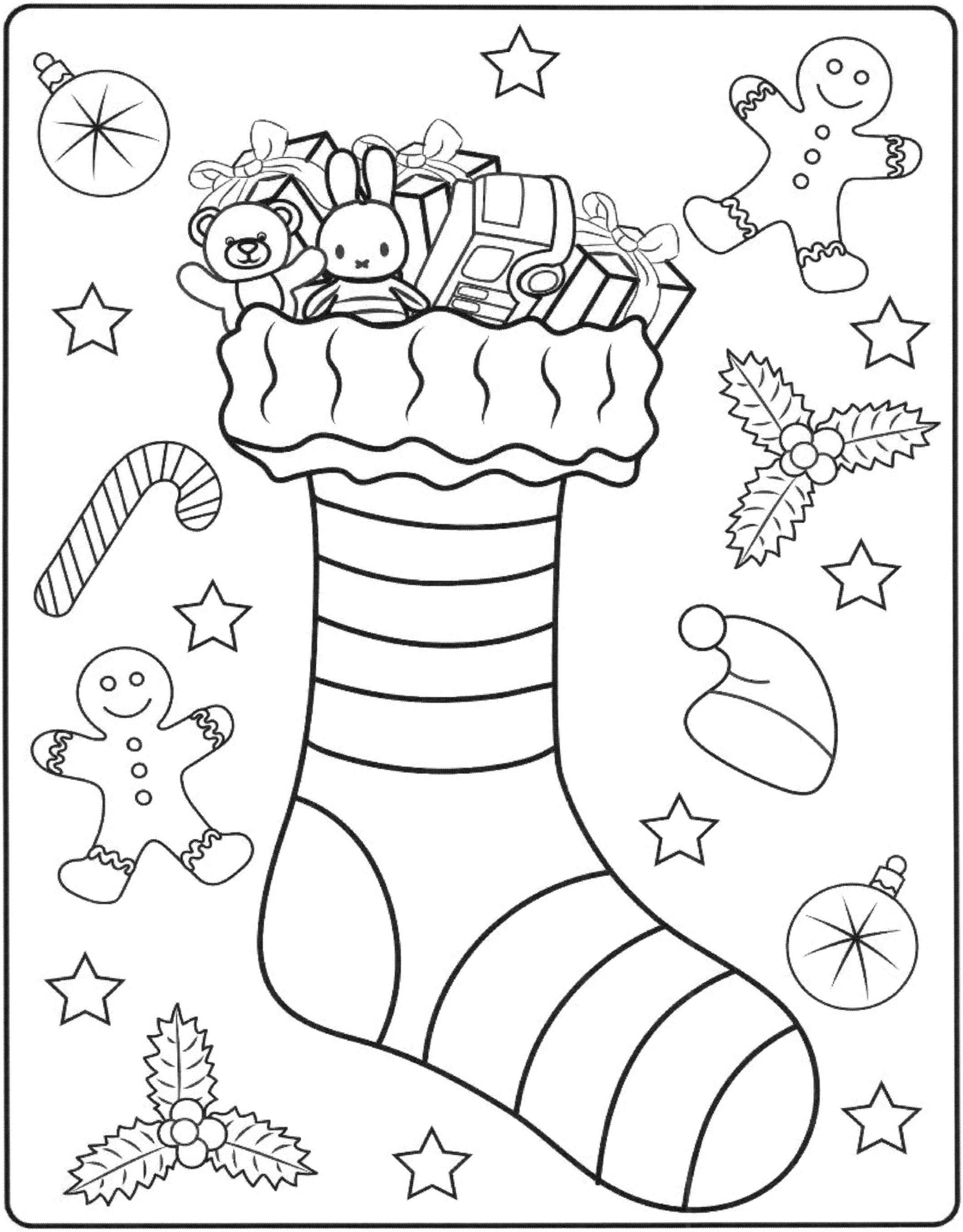

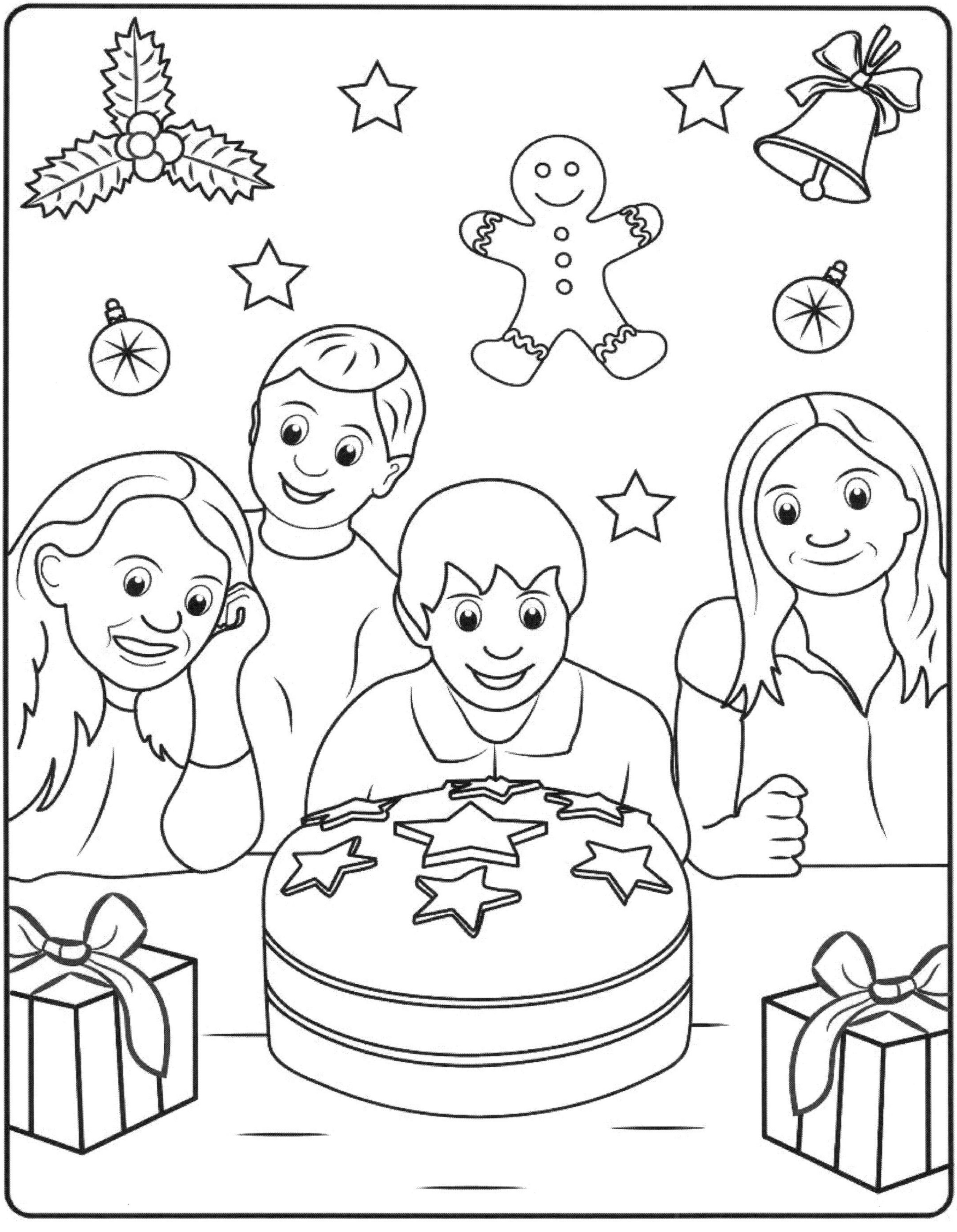

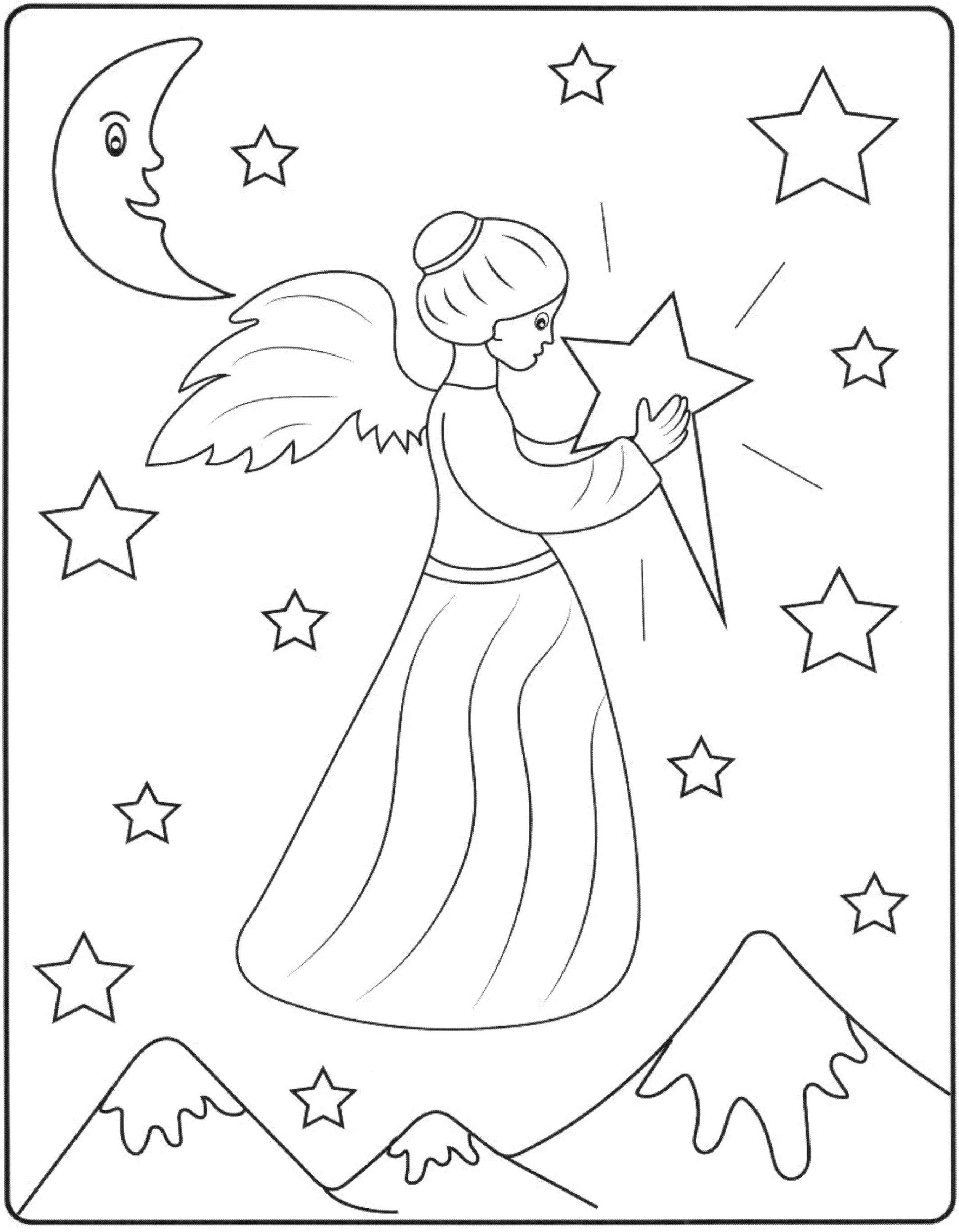

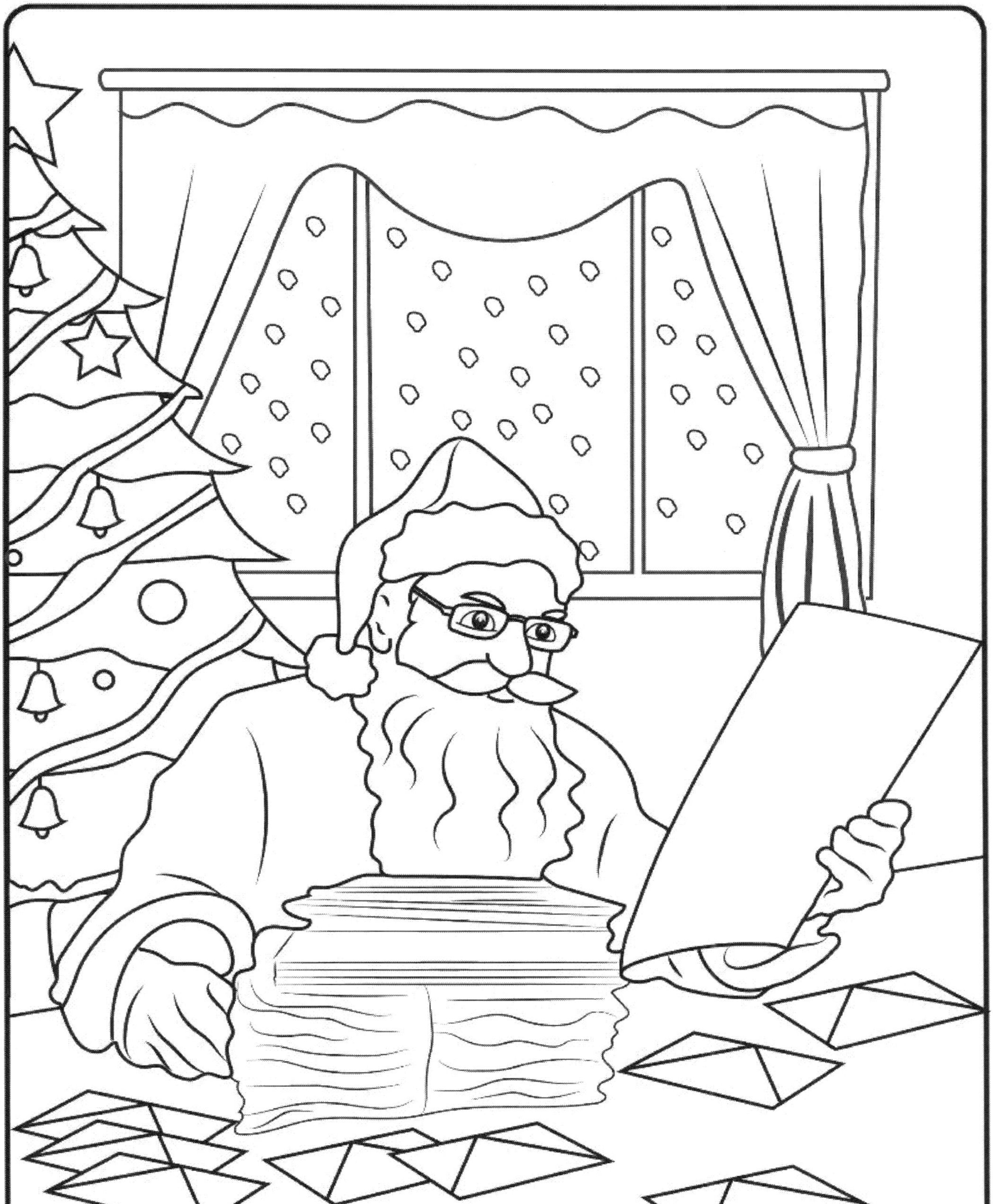

Dear Customer!

Thank you for your recent purchase, we hope you love it!

If you do, would you consider posting an online review?

This helps us to continue providing great products and helps potential buyers to make confident decisions.

Thank you in advance for your review and for being a preferred customer.

See more of my books!

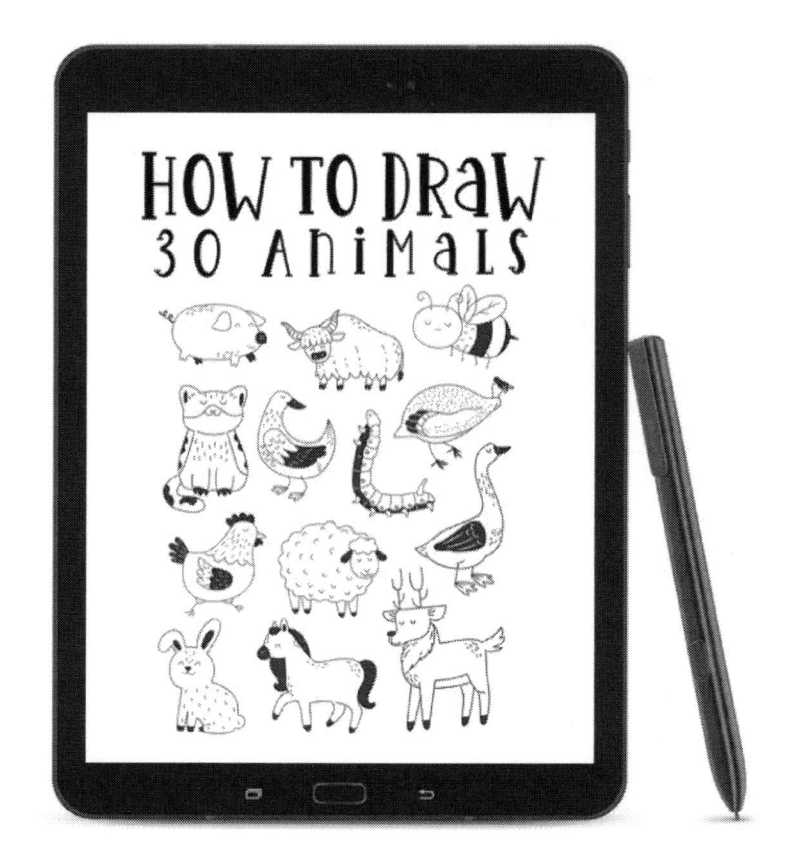

Michael Blackmore

FREE GIFT FOR YOU!

scan me!

Printed in Great Britain
by Amazon